SOME
COUNTRY
HOUSES
AND THEIR
OWNERS

*James
Lees-Milne*

Edited with an Introduction by
MICHAEL BLOCH

English 🐧 *Journeys*

PENGUIN BOOKS

Published by the Penguin Group
Penguin Books Ltd, 80 Strand, London WC2R ORL, England
Penguin Group (USA) Inc., 375 Hudson Street, New York, New York 10014, USA
Penguin Group (Canada), 90 Eglinton Avenue East, Suite 700, Toronto, Ontario, Canada M4P 2Y3
(a division of Pearson Penguin Canada Inc.)
Penguin Ireland, 25 St Stephen's Green, Dublin 2, Ireland
(a division of Penguin Books Ltd)
Penguin Group (Australia), 250 Camberwell Road, Camberwell, Victoria 3124, Australia
(a division of Pearson Australia Group Pty Ltd)
Penguin Books India Pvt Ltd, 11 Community Centre, Panchsheel Park, New Delhi – 110 017, India
Penguin Group (NZ), 67 Apollo Drive, Rosedale, North Shore 0632, New Zealand
(a division of Pearson New Zealand Ltd)
Penguin Books (South Africa) (Pty) Ltd, 24 Sturdee Avenue, Rosebank, Johannesburg 2196, South Africa

Penguin Books Ltd, Registered Offices: 80 Strand, London WC2R ORL, England

www.penguin.com

This selection first published 1975
Published in Penguin Books 2009

007

James Lees-Milne's original diary material © Michael Bloch 1975, 1977, 1983, 1985, 1994
Introductory and editorial material © Michael Bloch, 2009
All rights reserved

Set by Rowland Phototypesetting Ltd, Bury St Edmunds, Suffolk
Printed in England by Clays Ltd, St Ives plc

ISBN: 978-0-141-19090-7

www.greenpenguin.co.uk

MIX
Paper from
responsible sources
FSC
www.fsc.org   FSC™ C018179

Penguin Books is committed to a sustainable
future for our business, our readers and our planet.
This book is made from Forest Stewardship
Council™ certified paper.

ALWAYS LEARNING   **PEARSON**

Introduction

The National Trust is a private charity, a members' organization, and a property-owning body. (It has never been part of the government – though governments have generally approved of its aims and often taken measures to help it.) When it was founded in the 1890s, its main object was to acquire land in order to preserve and give public access to gems of the English landscape which were under threat from the expansion of suburbia. However, by the 1930s it recognized that equally in need of preservation were the many beautiful country houses, great and small, for which England was justly famous, together with their often splendid parks and art collections. Thanks to a long agricultural depression, the deaths of heirs in the First World War, and the vastly increased taxation of incomes and estates, most of their traditional owners, if they had not already abandoned them, looked as if they would be unable to continue living in them for much longer.

In 1936, the National Trust set up its Country Houses Scheme. Shorn of its complexities, the deal was that, if an owner donated his house to the Trust, preferably together with its estate and valuable contents, he would no longer have to face death duties on it, and he and his heirs could continue living in it as tenants paying a nominal rent. There were two further conditions. First, the Trust insisted on public access. This generally caused few problems, as many owners were already opening their houses to the public. Second, having no general funds out of which to maintain its properties, the Trust required that an owner donating his house also hand over an 'endowment', often amounting to a substantial fortune, to provide for future upkeep. This was a considerable disincentive to would-be donors (though the Trust, as a charity paying no tax, required less maintenance income than would a private owner).

The Scheme was run by a committee, mostly consisting of art-loving, public-spirited aristocrats, chaired by Lord Esher. As its secretary, the Country Houses Committee engaged a young man named James Lees-Milne (1908–97). Jim (as he was known) was handsome, courteous, intelligent and industrious. The son of a Worcestershire squire, brought up in a manor house, educated at Eton and Magdalen College, Oxford, he had an innate understanding of the country-house-owning class and how they needed to be handled if they were to part with their ancestral properties. To both his Committee and the owners he visited he appeared to be a gentle soul, but in fact he was sharply observant, extremely canny and somewhat manipulative.

During the three years before the Second World War, Jim visited numerous country house owners up and down the land who expressed interest in the Scheme. Many of them he befriended. However, few of them subscribed to the Scheme at the time. To most of them it seemed that they would be giving up a lot for very little. During the Scheme's first years, only owners who were either childless (such as Lord Lothian of Blickling), radically socialist in their views (such as Sir Charles Trevelyan of Wallington), or so rich that handing over a large house and endowment involved little sacrifice (such as Lord Astor of Cliveden), signed up to it.

Jim left his job for war service in 1939, but returned to it at the end of 1941 when he was invalided out of the army. The situation had now radically changed. Such were the upheavals that the war had brought about that few owners could envisage living in their houses again in the traditional way. Taxation had soared to confiscatory levels; domestic servants had disappeared; the houses themselves were often requisitioned for use by the armed services or various institutions, the owning families confined to a corner of them. Under these desperate conditions, many owners who had spurned the National Trust in the 1930s began to see it as the only body offering a solution which might preserve their ancestral estates and allow them to go on inhabiting at least parts of their houses. Also the need to 'endow' a house was no longer the burden it had been, the Country Houses Committee having decided that, for the duration of hostilities, only a minimum endowment would be required 'to keep the roof watertight and dry-rot at bay'.

In 1942, therefore, Jim – often experiencing wartime travel difficulties – again set out to visit owners who were interested in the Trust's Scheme. But there were two big differences. Whereas in 1936 most owners were merely curious about the Scheme, they were now often eager to transfer their properties under it without delay (though legal and financial complications usually meant that years might pass before such transfers were complete). And whereas Jim's visits to owners from 1936 to 1939 are only recorded in dry reports, from 1942 to 1945 he described them in a fascinating diary, which was published in the 1970s and remains in print, having been hailed both as a masterpiece of English literature and a contribution to social history. In it, Jim describes the dilapidated wartime condition of the houses and the privations (notably from lack of servants, fuel and food) suffered by their owners. But although he writes at a time of chaos and destruction, thanks to the owners' eccentricities the diary is often uproariously funny.

On 1 June 1945, Jim wrote:

The lengths to which I have gone, the depths which I have plumbed, the concessions which I have (once most reluctantly) granted to acquire properties for the National Trust, will not all be known by that ungrateful body. It might be shocked by the extreme zeal of its servant, if it did. Yet I like to think that the interest of the property, or building, rather than the Trust has been my objective. I have to guard against the collector's acquisitiveness.

The war ended in 1945; but until 1950, when he gave up full-time work for the National Trust, Jim continued to visit owners and write about them in his diary. He was indeed busier than ever during these years, as crippling taxes and a climate of social change resulted in many further offers of country houses to the Trust. The postwar Labour Government encouraged the process, presenting the Trust with a number of houses (the first was Cotehele) which it had accepted from the former owning families in lieu of death duties, and looking into ways of helping the Trust with the expense of maintaining its properties.

Many houses Jim visited during the 1940s, but by no means all, eventually became National Trust properties. For there were many factors which might frustate a would-be donor: lack of adequate endowment; legal problems (especially in the case of houses subject to family trusts); or simply the fact that the Country Houses Committee, advised by Jim, did not think a property worthy of acceptance. These selections from his diaries – which are in the form of an alphabetical gazetteer – are therefore divided into two parts. The first deals with those houses Jim visited which are now owned by the Trust – all of which can be visited, at times stated in the National Trust's annual *Handbook*, by its members for free or by the general public on payment of a charge. The second deals with those houses he saw and wrote about which did not pass to the Trust, of which some have been demolished or put to institutional use, but many (particularly where they are still owned by the families he visited) are also open to the public today.

James Lees-Milne's 1940s diaries were originally published in four volumes, with titles taken from Coleridge's poem 'Kubla Khan' – *Ancestral Voices* (1975), *Prophesying Peace* (1977), *Caves of Ice* (1983) and *Midway on the Waves* (1985). All are still available in the Clocktower Paperback series published by Michael Russell. But those who wish to read more may prefer to consult the recent one-volume edition – *Diaries, 1942–1954* – published by John Murray in hardback (2006) and paperback (2007).

PART ONE

Houses Now Owned by the National Trust

(years in which the houses became the National Trust's property given in brackets)

ANGLESEY ABBEY, *Cambridgeshire*
(1962)

Lord Fairhaven had transformed this property from a medieval ruin into a comfortable 1930s residence. Though he did not donate it to the National Trust until the 1960s, discussions began during the Second World War. He was one of the few owners J.L.-M. visited who managed, despite wartime restrictions, to continue leading a luxurious way of life.

10 September 1943

Was met at Cambridge and driven by the agent to Anglesey Abbey. On our arrival Lord Fairhaven was strutting in front of his porch, in too immaculate a blue suit, and watch in hand. He is a slightly absurd, vain man, egocentric, pontifical, and too much blessed with the world's goods. He is an enthusiastic amateur, yet ignorant of the arts he patronizes. At luncheon I was ravenous, having breakfasted at 7.30. Even so I did not eat as much as my host, who at forty-seven has a large paunch, a heavy jowl, pugnacious chin and mottled complexion. The nice agent, a gentleman from these parts (Lord Fairhaven is not from these parts), only spoke when spoken to. After luncheon he was dismissed and we strolled down the Lode bank into the garden. This is well kept in spite of the war. It has been laid out on eighteenth-century lines. Just before the war Fairhaven planted a long, straight line of limes, chestnuts and planes in four rows with caryatid statues by Coade of Lambeth at the far end. Unfortunately the vista does not begin from and so cannot be enjoyed from the house.

Anglesey Abbey is, like Packwood [House, Warwickshire], more a fake than not. The only genuine remains are the calefactorium, or crypt (used as a dining-room) dating from 1236, with thick, quadripartite ceiling of clunch, some medieval buttressed walls and the greatly restored 1600 south front. Lord Fairhaven put back the pointed gables and added the cresting to the porch. The interior is entirely his, opulent and pile-carpeted. But his new library with high coved ceiling, lined with books (first editions and un-cut), is fine. He has a desultory collection of good things that do not amount to a great collection. There is a corridor of Etty nudes in his private bedroom wing.

Exhausted, I had a bath and changed into a dark suit. Lord Fairhaven wore a dinner jacket. We had a four-course dinner of soup, lobster, chicken and savoury, waited on by a butler. Lord Fairhaven is served first, before his guests, in the feudal manner which only the son of an oil magnate would adopt. Presumably the idea is that in the event of the food being poisoned the host will gallantly succumb, and his instant death will be a warning to the rest of the table to abstain. Port and brandy followed.

25–26 January 1946
Got to Anglesey Abbey for tea. Wonderfully appointed house, soft-treading carpets; full of semi-works of art, over-heated, over-flowered, and I do not covet it or any-

thing in it. We had a frugal tea but sumptuous dinner prefaced by whisky and epilogued by port. Lord Fairhaven is precise, complacent and dogmatic. Hospitable and kind, though aloof and pleased with his noble position. Who is he, anyway? The son of an American oil magnate. We talked till midnight and groaned delightedly about the way the nation is going to the dogs. Woke with slight hangover from whisky and port, and my over-heated bedroom. The chauffeur who has two Rolls-Royces here discovered my clutch was slipping and put it right for me.

ATTINGHAM PARK, *Shropshire*
(1947)

The owner, Lord Berwick, was dominated by his wife, who was determined that he should leave the property to the National Trust.

7–8 July 1943
From Evesham to Shrewsbury by train, changing at Hartlebury to the Severn Valley line. What a beautiful valley it is, with gently sloping wooded banks and miniature scenery, even on a grey day. I stayed two nights with the Berwicks at Attingham. They inhabit a fraction of the east wing. The WAAFs occupy the rest of the house. The Ministry of Works has at my instigation protected the principal rooms by boarding up the fireplaces and even dados. The uniform Pompeian red of the walls is I presume contemporary, that is to say

late eighteenth-century. In my bathroom the walls were papered with Captain Cook scenery just like the upstairs bedroom at Laxton [Hall, Northamptonshire]. The first night we had champagne to celebrate Attingham's survival to date. After dinner I read through the 1827 Sale Catalogue of contents, many of which the 3rd Lord Berwick, then Minister to the Court at Naples, bought from his elder brother the 2nd Lord.

[The following day] Lady Berwick and I went to tea at Cronkhill, one of the houses on the estate, built by John Nash in 1810. It was designed in the romantic style of an Italian villa, and is the precursor of many similar Victorian villas. Lady Berwick behaves towards her neighbours with a studied affability, a queenly graciousness which must be a trifle intimidating to those upon whom it is dispensed.

After tea I walked with Lord Berwick in the deer park having been enjoined by his wife to talk seriously about Attingham's future, and press him for a decision on various points. I did not make much progress in this respect. On the other hand he expanded in a strangely endearing way. When alone he loosens up and is quite communicative. All the seeming silliness and nervousness vanish. He talked to me earnestly of the ghosts that have been seen at Attingham by the WAAFs. Lady Berwick would not have tolerated this nonsense, had she been present. He kept stopping and anxiously looking over his shoulder lest she might be overhearing him, but he did not stand stock still and revolve, which he does in the drawing room when she starts talking business. He told me that Lady Sibyl Grant, his neighbour at

Pitchford [Hall], constantly writes to him on the forbidden subject, passing on advice as to health which she has been given by her spiritual guides. She no longer dares telephone this information for fear, so Lord Berwick asserted, of the spirits hearing and taking offence, but more likely for fear of Lady Berwick overhearing and strongly disapproving. He is not the least boring about his psychical beliefs but is perplexed by the strange habits of ghosts. He asked me, did I think it possible that one could have been locked in the housemaid's cupboard? And why should another want to disguise itself as a vacuum cleaner? Really, he is a delicious man.

17 March 1944
Forsyth [an architect] motored me to Attingham where I stayed the night. I walked into the deer park looking for Lord Berwick. Found him exercising his little dog, Muffet. He talks to me far more confidently than he used to. I think he is one of the most endearing men I have ever met – feckless, helpless and courteous. We had a good dinner of four courses, including chicken and burgundy. Lady Sibyl Grant said of him, 'Poor Tom, he should not have lived in this age. He cannot drive a car, ride a bicycle, fish or shoot. He would have stepped in and out of a sedan chair so beautifully.'

30 May 1947
We found Attingham [which the ailing Lord Berwick was letting, with the National Trust's encouragement, to Shropshire Adult College] a scene of Russian tragedy.

Lady Berwick was hollow-eyed and miserable. Once or twice I thought she was in tears. They are fast selling contents and clearing out of the house for the College. They will withdraw to the small east wing. Lord Berwick was wheeled up to us in a chair. He is a shrunken, almost inhuman bundle incapable of moving hand or limb. He speaks lower and slower, and is most piteous. She thinks he may die at any moment. [He did so a few weeks later, bequeathing Attingham to the Trust.] Two nurses are in perpetual attendance and I suspect make the Bs poorer than ever. I drove away laden with the posts of Caroline Murat's bed which the Berwicks are selling at Sotheby's.

BLICKLING HALL, *Norfolk*
(1940)

The National Trust unexpectedly inherited this great Jacobean palace when its owner Lord Lothian died while serving as British Ambassador to Washington in 1940.

14 May 1942

On arrival at Blickling we are greeted by a sea of Nissen huts in the park in front of the Orangery, and a brick NAAFI construction opposite the entry to the house. The sudden view of the south front takes the breath away. We walk round the outside. Then Lord Lothian's secretary, now our housekeeper-caretaker, conducts me round those state rooms on the first floor that are not occupied by the RAF. The furniture has now been removed to Henley Hall for safety; the best pictures removed too. The RAF are in Miss O'Sullivan's bad books for they have needlessly broken several windows, and smashed the old crown glass. They have forced the locks of the doors into the state rooms, out of devilry. This sort of thing is inevitable.

5–6 August 1942

I wanted to see the mausoleum at Blickling, so Forsyth and I walked across the park to it. It is a squat pyramid designed by Joseph Bonomi in 1793. Very solid and well constructed, surrounded by thin iron railings. We found that the padlock had been forced and the gate opened. Also the extremely heavy door of the mausoleum was ajar. It too had been forced and even bent. Considerable strength must have been required to do this, and possibly the use of one of several tree trunks lying in the bracken. Within three deeply splayed recesses are sarcophagi of marble, the central one of the 2nd Earl of Buckingham-shire, the side ones his two countesses'. The left sar-cophagus had been hacked with a blunt instrument, and the marble coating prised off the side. Evidently the culprits are the RAF boys who have tried to break open the sarcophagus, believing they would find inside the body of the second countess, who is reputed to have been buried wearing all her jewellery.

It is wonderful being responsible to the committee for Blickling. I am in love with the house, garden, park and estate. In spite of the RAF station, Blickling seems to be at the furthermost extremity of East Anglia, even of England.

At the end of the war J.L.-M., hoping to make progress with his book on the architect Robert Adam, took a holiday at Blickling, which was still largely occupied by the RAF. He stayed with Miss O'Sullivan in her quarters and worked in the great library.

24 June 1945

I am blissfully happy this afternoon. I write this at my table on the raised platform at the south-east end of the Gallery, as I had for so long pictured myself doing, surrounded by 12,000 calf-bound books, looking on to the beautiful but unkempt, unmown garden, and Ivory's temple at the far end of the vista. Here I intend to work for a fortnight, and pray to God no distractions will prevent me. But my character is weak, and I bow before temptation. I sleep and breakfast in Miss O'Sullivan's flat in the wing; I take all my other meals at the inn, where the landlady Mrs O'Donoghue is my friend. It is a warm sunny day. The air smells of roses and pinks. The tranquillity accentuates the extreme remoteness of Blickling, this beautiful house which I love.

BROCKHAMPTON, *Herefordshire*
(1946)

Left to the National Trust by its heirless owner Colonel Lutley.

27 December 1946

Papa and I drove to Brockhampton near Bromyard in the morning where we met Admiral and Mrs Bevir [Secretary of the NT and wife], Ruby and Christopher

Holland-Martin [NT Treasurer and brother], and Colin Jones [NT official]. Lunched in the cold, cold hall and walked round the house where Colonel Lutley's personal belongings are left lying about since the day he died. Something poignant in a house which has suddenly ceased to exist with the last owner. Life arrested in old tobacco jars with the lids off, smelly old pipes, books turned face downwards on tables, the well-worn favourite chair with deep imprint of the late 'behind' and threadbare arms, and the mournful, reproachful gaze of dozens of forgotten ancestors on the walls. Estate, house and contents all left to the National Trust. The house, which has a situation of unparalleled Midlands beauty overlooking valley and woods, could be made decent by the removal of Victorian trimmings round the windows, and the installation of sash-bars. No furniture of museum quality but very nice plain utility Georgian, as genuine as the old squires who for centuries loved it. Two good Georgian bookcases. The Admiral being incredibly muddleheaded and Ruby as friendly as a swordfish can be. Ruby who drove over in a luxurious Bentley produced a luncheon basket with fittings like a bar, complete with gin and whisky and coffee. Papa and I rather humbly drank our milk. The dear old butler with his sweet, sad smile is stone deaf and speaks in a whisper. The housekeeper, dignified and courteous like the one at Chesney Wold [in Dickens's *Bleak House*], speaks like a BBC announcer. Papa and I drove down to Lower Brockhampton and examined this little black-and-white manor and gatehouse with enthusiasm. It is just the sort of house my father cares for.

16 June 1947

Motored to Brockhampton, arriving in the cool of the evening. How beautiful this place is. I walked down to Lower Brockhampton just before dark, the trees dead quiet, not even whispering, and the undergrowth steaming. Two enormous black-and-white bulls gave me a fright by noiselessly poking their great faces over a gate and peering at me in a meditative manner. This evening the whole tragedy of England impressed itself upon me. This small, not very important seat, in the heart of our secluded country, is now deprived of its last squire. A whole social system has broken down. What will replace it beyond government by the masses, uncultivated, rancorous, savage, philistine, the enemies of all things beautiful? How I detest democracy. More and more I believe in benevolent autocracy.

BUSCOT PARK, *Oxfordshire*
(1949)

Donated to the National Trust by Lord Faringdon, the raffish socialist heir to a banking fortune.

20 December 1946

At three we reached Buscot. Gavin Faringdon showed us the outside, all kept in apple-pie order. A lovely walled garden in a hollow. The Harold Peto path from the SE angle of the house towards the lake is impressive. The house is a well-contrived fake. Paul Hyslop [architect in the classical tradition] has done very well, I think. Gavin certainly has some first-rate furniture and pictures. House well appointed and heated. The Admiral [NT Sec. Admiral Bevir] bewildered by Gavin's socialism-cum-plutocracy, as well he might be. Gavin has a youngish, ogling, rather raddled American staying, or rather living with him. For dinner Gerald Berners [the composer-aesthete Lord Berners], Robert Heber-Percy [his boy-friend] and another young man came over [from nearby Faringdon House]. Poor Admiral more bewildered than ever by the company. His incredulous eyes out on stalks. His instincts offended. I did not enhance my credibility by talking too much about art and drama. He was well out of his depth and kept trying desperately to surface like a moribund dolphin. When the Faringdon House party left Gavin kept us sitting up till long past midnight in spite of poor Admiral's unrepressed yawns.

CHARLECOTE PARK, *Warwickshire*
(1946)

This Elizabethan house near Stratford-on-Avon, in whose park the young Shakespeare reputedly shot deer, was donated to the National Trust by the children of the eccentric Sir Henry Fairfax-Lucy after his death in 1944.

18 July 1942
From Warwick station I was driven to Charlecote Park. It is the second time that I have been there; the first was in 1936, which shows how long negotiations have been dragging on. On that occasion I was sent to consider

and report upon the merits of the house. Sir Henry Fairfax-Lucy, military, dapper and arrogant walked me quickly round the park and garden. It was a rainy day, I remember. On returning to the porch, whence we had set out immediately on my arrival, Sir Henry stretched out his hand and bade me good-bye. In those days I was shy. Nervously I asked if I might see inside. The reply was, 'There is absolutely no need. Charlecote is known to be one of the great, the greatest houses of England. Good morning.' So without disputing I went off with my tail between my legs. On my return to the office I was told I had been a fool.

Now as for Sir Henry Fairfax-Lucy, today I have found out about him. He may be a pompous ass like Justice Shallow (who was supposed to be Sir Thomas Lucy), but underneath the strutting, the peppery, the arrogant surface, a kindly old man lurks. In fact I am rather sorry for him, because I think he is a little odd. He is obstinate and muddle-headed because of his oddness. I believe he struggles to be reasonable, and just cannot manage to be. His ideas do not co-ordinate. His lisp is like that of a peevish child eating pap.

We went inside the house this time; and then round the park, again in the rain. He showed me the complicated boundaries of the land he proposes to make over. But he kept contradicting himself so that neither he nor I knew at the end of his visit what his intentions were. Although most indefinite he was most exacting. He was also very cheese-paring, reducing the total income the Trust should receive to shillings and pence as well as pounds. I thought he was rather touching when he urged haste – how is this to be achieved with him? – if we wanted the transaction to go through. 'I don't want to say anything unseemly, but Lady Lucy is very seriously ill.' The place is of course hers, not his.

31 May 1945
Motored to Charlecote, picking up Clifford Smith [furniture expert] at Leamington Spa station. Brian [Fairfax-Lucy] was his smiling and helpful self, but the agent an obstructive ass. Clifford's hesitant enthusiasms were constantly unleashed at the wrong moment, and so delayed progress in outdoor consultations. I had to chivvy him indoors where he properly belongs. Today we examined the Brewery, with its vats and implements, all of which can be revived; and the harness room with its rows of brightly kept bridles and bits, and the coachouses stuffed with Victorian buggies, spiders and barouches. I urged the family to save and leave [to the Trust] these things, for they will make a fascinating exhibit to future generations who will not have known the world in which they played an everyday part.

Clifford and I discovered in the gatehouse, the stables and disused servants' hall several ancient pieces of furniture, notably the hall table of great length, another Elizabethan table and a Queen Anne walnut veneered table which must have been thrown out during the last century. We are going to have them brought back. The house was too drastically altered in the 1850s. The strange thing is that Mrs George Lucy, who perpetrated the abominations, was the one member of the family who loved Charlecote and revered its Shakespearean associations.

Yet she over-restored the house out of all recognition, and introduced furniture and fabrics, like napkins, which she pretended Shakespeare and Queen Elizabeth saw and used. The ability of righteous people to deceive themselves always amazes me.

The Gatehouse, forecourt garden and stables form an extremely picturesque group. The park, with deer and sheep, the Avon below the library window, the flat meadows on the far bank, the long lime avenue, make Charlecote a dream of slumbering beauty.

CHARTWELL, *Kent*
(1946)

Winston Churchill's house in the Weald was bought by his friends after the Second World War and presented to the National Trust on condition that he could continue living there undisturbed until his death.

23 November 1949

Motored Johnnie Churchill [Winston's artist nephew who had been J.L.-M.'s best friend at Oxford] to Chartwell this morning. Mr and Mrs Winston were in London so we were able to go where we wanted. It must once have been a nice Queen Anne house, but Mr C. has altered it out of all recognition, and it is now quite ugly; but of course bears his strong impress. We saw his study and adjoining bedroom. If all the photographs and pictures and framed letters from Marlborough, and from himself to General Alexander and others, remain, Chartwell will be interesting to posterity. His bedroom is rather austere in spite of windows on all sides and three telephones by the bed. The view from it is splendid – the great lake made by him and the dam, which I remember him constructing when I stayed here twenty years ago, and the chain of pools in the topmost of which water is pumped by machine from the bottom lake. What a to-do went on during these operations, Mr C., clad in waders, standing up to his chest in mud and shouting directions like Napoleon before Austerlitz. The long downstairs room is now full of his paintings, of which the earlier ones in the style of Sickert, without the later ubiquitous blue, are not too bad. We looked at Johnnie's slate frieze [of the Battle of Blenheim] being installed in the loggia. Johnnie is a dear old friend and we had a great gossip about his family. He says he doesn't care for Christopher Soames but does like Duncan Sandys [W.C.'s sons-in-law]. Mr C. has cultivated a deafness which he turns on like a tap when he is bored: an excellent form of defence and one adopted by many old people to whom time is precious. Chartwell is fascinating as the shrine of a great man, just as Hughenden is. The moment I set foot in the house I said to Johnnie, 'I have not been here since Oxford days and I vividly remember the smell of the house. What is it?' 'Cigars and brandy', he said. Of course. It is far from disagreeable, rather like cedar wood. Agreeable, I suppose, because his cigars are expensive ones.

CLIVEDEN, *Berkshire*
(1942)

Reserving the right for himself and his family to continue living there, Viscount Astor donated his Thames-side palace (later to achieve notoriety as the place where Jack Profumo met Christine Keeler, and now a hotel) to the National Trust during the Second World War.

19 May 1943
A very hot day at Cliveden. The site over the river is, as John Evelyn observed in the seventeenth century, superb. The house too is well worthy of the Trust. It illustrates the very end of the Palladian tradition. Barry conceived it with a real regard for architectural principles. It is heavy and majestical outside. The interior, altered by the architect J. L. Pearson in the nineties, has very little distinction. The Astors were away and I went inside. The famous Orkney tapestries have been taken down. The pictures, including the Reynoldses, were hanging, for the greater part of the house is still in use by the family. The splendid gardens are unkempt.

24 February 1948
Called on Bill Astor [the heir]. I persuaded him to write and ask his father to agree to the house being opened at least one afternoon this season. I pressed that the public could not be expected to understand how Lord Astor found this impossible.

CLOUDS HILL, *Dorset*
(1945)

Home of 'Lawrence of Arabia'.

20 September 1945

Clouds Hill, T. E. Lawrence's cottage, is in the middle of Bovington Heath, which is a blasted waste of desolation, churned feet-deep in mud by a thousand army tanks. The cottage is embowered in rhododendrons. It is a pathetic shoddy little place. The visitors have stolen all they could lay their hands on, including the screw of the porthole window in Lawrence's bedroom, and the clasps of the other windows. The bunk gives an idea of his asceticism. Pat Knowles, his batman, is back from abroad. He and his wife, a pretty, gazelle-like woman, live in another cottage across the way where Lawrence fed with them. They conduct visitors over Clouds Hill, and dare not let them out of their sight for a minute. Knowles is a high-minded, cultivated proletarian, a youngish 45 with vestiges of gold hair. Bespectacled face not a bit puffy, but must once have been handsome.

COTEHELE, *Cornwall*
(1947)

This wonderfully preserved house, owned for five centuries by the ancestors of Lord Mount Edgcumbe, was the first English property to be accepted by the Treasury in part-payment of death duties and presented by them to the National Trust.

7 December 1946

Very showery but beautiful day. After breakfast motored across the Tamar into Cornwall, up and down narrow lanes and up steep hills until I reached Cotehele, which faces east over Calstock and the river. Were it moved just a little further southward the house would be better situated. Then it would overlook the lovely ribbon loop of the river. As it is, the situation is romantic, wild and wooded. The caretaker was away with the key, but the farmer's wife most kindly motored to fetch the daily help from Calstock who had another key. This kind and intelligent woman showed me round the house which is fully furnished. Meanwhile the old coachman, seeing my motor, came and talked. Told me that until 1939 he drove a 1911 Rolls for Lord Mount Edgcumbe. He expressed himself very concerned about my 'points'. He left and presently returned, wearing a topcoat with velvet collar and old-fashioned billycock, to present me with the distributor points of his old Rolls. I was charmed by him. Didn't know what to do with object presented.

Cotehele House is not striking from the outside, being squat and spread. It is actually far larger than one is led to suppose from the front, for it has two courtyards. It is uniformly old, late medieval with pointed windows, all of granite. The great hall is as fine as any I have seen, with curved windbraces in the roof and plastered white-washed walls, hung with armour. In the oldest wing all the rooms are panelled, walls plastered and the

Stuart furniture upholstered in needlework, none later than the eighteenth century. The contents are un-touched, superb. Indeed it is a superb house.

7–8 May 1947
At midday I left for Cornwall. The luxurious train jour-ney dispersed my choler. I reached Gunnislake at 7.30 and Cotehele at 8 for dinner. Lord Mount Edgcumbe is in bed with a temperature, but his Countess, a little, gentle, sweet and pathetic old lady, was about. Their story is a tragic one. They inherited during the war, and their only son was killed at Dunkirk. They are now packing up to leave Cotehele which since the thirteenth century has been in their family. I am given a bedroom at the top of the entrance gate-tower, approaching by a twisting stone staircase, and in isolation.

Slept ill: lightning during the night which flashed through my casements and lit up the great tower and courtyard. I worked all day in the state rooms, listing those contents which the NT would like and a few things to be got rid of. Most of the contents are very good indeed, if only they were not so sadly perished. These state rooms are of the class of the Knole ones and this house is a miniature Knole of the West. It is so remote that I do not suppose great numbers will visit it. I hope not. There are two rather bedint [common], virginal sisters staying to help the Mount Edgcumbes pack. At first their vapid giggling annoyed me, but now I quite like them. Lady Mount E.'s cairn puppy has eaten a chunk out of the Turkey-work Queen Anne settee, and she thinks it rather naughty, that's all. There are a butler and some charming servants, all of the old school. The splendid Mt E.s, having lost their son and heir, are taking to live with them their unknown heir and his wife, who are New Zealanders.

COUGHTON COURT, *Warwickshire*
(1946)

The owner, Sir Robert Throckmorton, was not especially keen to hand over this important house but was influenced to do so by his formidable mother (the Lady Throckmorton referred to).

15 September 1942

Lady Throckmorton asked me to Coughton for the night, to go through the list of family heirlooms with her. She is living in the south wing only. The rest of the house is empty, in expectation of American officers, or nuns.

Lady Throckmorton is delightful: plain, unfashionable, intelligent and downright. *Très grande dame*. She has worked in Coughton's interests for thirty years, upholding the Catholic tradition, without becoming a Catholic herself. It is entirely owing to her that Coughton is to become Trust property, in the face of seemingly insuperable obstacles raised by the entail and the hostility of the Throckmorton family.

Coughton is a thoroughly romantic house, though I must say the late Georgian front is gloomy. There is something unconvincing and drab about thin rendering which peels. The central Perpendicular tower and the half-timbered wings are beautiful, as well as picturesque. The family associations – the papistry, recusancy, Gunpowder Plot and intermarriages with other ancient Catholic families – are thrilling.

FELBRIGG HALL, *Norfolk*
(1950s)

Bequeathed to the Trust by its childless ancestral owner, the antiquarian Wyndham Ketton-Cremer.

2–3 May 1942

The rector motored me part of the way to Felbrigg. I walked down the drive carrying my bag. Ketton-Cremer was not in when I arrived but his manservant, Ward, gave me tea. I later learned that only Ward and his wife 'do'. K.-C. spends most nights at his mother's house, and the daytime here. Then Ketton-Cremer came in. He is big and shapeless, ugly, mild and podgy. He carries his head on one side, and is wan and delicate. He is donnish, extremely cultivated and an urbane and polished writer. He is a trifle ill at ease rather than shy, yet punctilious, methodical and determined. If one let fall unconsidered opinions, he would not leave them unpicked-over, I feel sure. Toryish, if not prejudiced in his views of conduct. Yet open-minded and friendly in a cautious way. Very courteous too. His conversation, though measured and correct, is informative and agreeable. Oh, a most sympathetic man.

[After tea the following day] Ketton-Cremer read me

his will from beginning to end, asking for comments. Since the will covered foolscap sheet after sheet, and like all legal documents had no punctuation whatever, and the fire in the hall where we sat was hot, I kept dropping off. Politely K.-C. would throw me a deprecatory glance, and continue: 'And such Trust moneys may be invested in or laid out or applied in the subscription or purchase of or at interest upon the security of such stocks funds shares securities or other properties holdings or investments of whatsoever nature and wheresoever as my Trustees shall in their absolute discretion . . .' Pause, and another interrogative glance. 'That sounds perfectly satisfactory', I would say with too little conviction before nodding off again.

14 September 1946
Went on to Felbrigg for dinner. Wyndham Ketton-Cremer's mother staying, a sweet, white-haired old lady. Although physically flaccid he is mentally stimulating. Plenty of serious talk. House huge, but Wyndham is well looked after by his couple, and lives comfortably. No electric light, and I had to walk miles with a candle from my bedroom to the w.c. at the far end of the Stuart wing.

FENTON HOUSE, *Hampstead*
(1945)

A fine seventeenth-century merchant's house with a walled garden.

22 December 1944

I drove to Hampstead, to Fenton House, which belongs to Lady Binning, an elderly, delicate hot-housey lady. Fenton House was built in 1693 of beautiful red brick and has wrought-iron gates of the period. It is large for London, and has a large walled garden. Much of the pine wainscoting has been stripped by Lady Binning. She intends to leave her excellent furniture, and wishes the house to be a museum, but I feel it ought to be put to some use. Her porcelain collection is first-rate and at present bequeathed to the V&A, but she is prepared to alter her will. She gave me tea, and we liked each other, I fancy. At the end of tea she disclosed that she was anti-democratic and very pro-Nazi. She denied that the Germans had committed atrocities, and declared that the Jews were the root of all evil. Oh dear!

GUNBY HALL, *Lincolnshire*
(1944)

One of the houses which J.L.-M. was most proud of securing for the National Trust.

25 March 1943

When I told Eddy today that I was going this afternoon to stay at Gunby Hall in Lincolnshire, with Field Marshal Sir Archibald Montgomery-Massingberd, he could not believe his ears. Could there possibly be such a man? Indeed the Field Marshal received me in his study. He is tall, large, a little ponderous, handsome and impressive;

yet very gentle and kind. Lady Massingberd is slim, grey, jolly and also kind. They are Peter Montgomery's [an Eton friend of J.L.-M.] uncle and aunt on both his father and mother's sides of the family and are very fond of him; but because he has not yet married they are leaving him out of any settlement of Gunby they may make. The house is 1700, symmetrical, of secondary size, and of deep-plum brick with stone dressings. Every room and passage within has simple contemporary panelling. It was built by the Massingberds and is full of their portraits, including two Reynoldses. Now the Air Ministry is threatening to fell all the trees in the park and demolish the house, both in direct line of a runway which they have constructed without previously ascertaining the proximity of these obstacles. If the threats can be averted with our help, the Montgomery-Massingberds are ready to make the property over to the Trust straight away. They are such dear people that even if the house were worthless I would walk to the ends of the earth to help them.

A plain dinner with only water to drink. Wine and spirits are put away for patriotic motives. Hot water cut off for the same reason. Otherwise the house is full of servants, including a butler and pantry boy and four gardeners. Of course they revel in their imposed suffering. I wish I did.

14 June 1945
To Gunby for the night. The Field Marshal extremely pleased to see me. The old man has become rather more ponderous and slow. [The following morning] I walked

with him round the estate, visiting employees, paying their wages and collecting their savings funds from them. This estate is extraordinarily feudal, and has an air of wellbeing and content. The cottages are all very spick and span and the inmates on the best of terms with the Field Marshal. He has a habit of stopping and turning to me whenever he has something to say, which delays progress. He is very concerned about the election [which was about to bring Attlee's Labour Government to power]. I have never since a child seen such large and succulent strawberries as the Gunby ones. We ate them with honey, far better than sugar, and cream. Although the war is over there is [still] no alcohol in this house.

HAM HOUSE, *Richmond, Surrey*
(1947)

This was one of two historically important houses in the London area (the other was Osterley) which were eventually accepted by the National Trust with government support to be managed by the Victoria & Albert Museum.

19 March 1943

This afternoon I took the tube to Richmond, and thence a bus to Petersham. I walked down the long drive to Ham House. The grounds are indescribably overgrown and unkempt. I walked round the house, which appeared thoroughly deserted, searching for an entrance. The garden and front doors looked as though they had not been used for decades. So I returned to the back door and pulled a bell. Several seconds later a rusty tinkling echoed from distant subterranean regions. While waiting I recalled the grand ball given for Nefertiti Bethell which I attended in this house some ten years ago or more. The door was roughly jerked open, the bottom grating against the stone floor. The noise was accompanied by heavy breathing from within. An elderly man of sixty stood before me. He had red hair and a red face, carrot and port wine. He wore a tail coat and a starched shirt front which had come apart from the waistcoat. 'The old alcoholic family butler', I said to myself. Without asking my name or business, he said, 'Follow me.' Slowly he led me down a dark passage, his legs moving in painful jerks. At last he stopped outside a door, and knocked nervously. An ancient voice cried, 'Come in!' The seedy butler then said to me, 'Daddy is expecting you', and left me. I realized that he was the bachelor son of Sir Lyonel Tollemache, aged eighty-nine. As I entered the ancient voice said, 'You can leave us alone, boy!'

Sir Lyonel was sitting on an upright chair. He was dressed, unlike his son, immaculately in a grey suit, beautifully pressed, and wore a stock tie with a large pearl pin. I think he had spats over black polished shoes. A decorative figure, and courteous. He asked me several questions about the National Trust's scheme for preserving country houses, before ringing the bell and handing me back to his son.

The son showed me hurriedly round the house, which is melancholy in the extreme. All the rooms are dirty and dusty. The furniture and pictures have been moved to the country for safety. There is no doubt whatever

that, even without the contents, this house is worthy of
acceptance because of the superlative interior treatment,
the panelling, the exquisite parquetry floors, the extraordinary chimneypieces, the great staircase of pierced
balusters, the velvet hangings, etc. It is a wonderful
seventeenth-century house, and from the south windows
the garden layout of symmetrical beds, stone gate plinths
and ironwork is superb. Once we were away from the
father, whom he clearly holds in mortal dread, the son
became confidential. He said the family were worth
£2 million and did not receive as much as sixpence in
each pound; that they had two gardeners instead of
twelve, and no indoor servants except a cook (and himself). He told me he was so distracted by looking after
the Ham property and the Lincolnshire estate that at
times he felt suicidal. I looked straight at him, and knew
that the poor man meant it. When I waved goodbye,
the faintest flicker of a smile crossed his bucolic face, and
a tiny tear was on his cheek.

HUGHENDEN, *Buckinghamshire*
(1946)

*The house of the Victorian prime minister Benjamin Disraeli,
which showed his love of the Gothic.*

26 March 1944
I drove Stuart [Preston, an American soldier friend of
J.L.-M.] to Hughenden. Mrs Langley-Taylor received us
in the new wing built forty years ago by Coningsby

Disraeli, Dizzy's nephew and heir. I recall being brought here in about 1930 from Oxford, and being received by Coningsby Disraeli in the library. He was wearing a dusty velvet skull cap and, if I remember right, a blue velvet jacket and string bow tie. The main part of the house is at present used by the RAF for target-spotting, and cannot be entered. Mrs Langley-Taylor told me that after the war nearly every room will be furnished for show, and that Major Abbey when he bought the property [to preserve it as a national monument] also bought the Disraeli contents. Hughenden will make a splendid and interesting National Trust property for three reasons – its historic associations, its mid-Victorian architecture and furnishing, and its amenity on the outskirts of horrid High Wycombe. The park is beautiful and well maintained. Some fine trees, and the garden laid out in Victorian parterres with plenty of terracotta urns and insipid statuary of cherubs and angels, now put away, which Queen Mary called 'sugar babies' when she visited the place. I was delighted with Hughenden. It is deliciously hideous. Disraeli stripped it of its white stucco, revealed the red brick, and added the ugly window surrounds and crenellations. Mrs Langley-Taylor showed us Disraeli's bedroom, which is now her own. She says Lady Desborough [the society hostess, then in her eighties] remembers being patted on the head by Disraeli here, and being repelled by his greasy black curls.

KEDLESTON, *Derbyshire*
(1986)

When J.L.-M. visited this architectural masterpiece, formerly owned by the great imperialist Lord Curzon and now by his nephew Lord Scarsdale, it was not as a National Trust official but as the author of a book on its principal architect, Robert Adam. Only forty years later was Kedleston to come to the National Trust, after the government had agreed to provide the massive endowment required to maintain it. J.L.-M.'s description is of interest in showing what five years of army occupation had done to a great house.

26 May 1945

I caught a midday train to Derby. Found a taxi and drove to Kedleston. Down the long drive there suddenly bursts upon the vision the great house, best seen from the Adam bridge. It is very grand, very large and symmetrical from this side, the north. The two pavilions are plastered and coloured ruddy brown. The centre block is of severe, dark Derbyshire stone. Lord Curzon, with his sense of the magnificent, erected the screen of Adamesque railings, the great gates and overthrows to form the forecourt, now overgrown with grass. At the entrance to these gates is a series of army huts with a little suburban garden in front of each. Again, all over the park are unsightly poles and wires, something to do with radio location. The two north pavilions, designed by Brettingham and built by Paine, are in themselves quite large houses, at least large enough to command a respectable park for themselves. The south side is disappointing, for poor Adam has again been roughly treated here. His two additional pavilions were never carried out. His beautiful centre block and dome, so full of movement and grace, is not given a fair chance, with the tiresome poplars in front of the east pavilion, and the west hidden by scrubby little trees. Also the parish church should not have been left where it is, enveloped by the house like a rat by a boa constrictor.

Lord Scarsdale's mother greeted me at the door of the east pavilion where the family live. The Army are occupying the west pavilion. The centre block is unoccupied, and under dust sheets. Whereas Lord Curzon thought he was pigging it with only thirty indoor servants, today they have one woman for three hours each morning. The mother is living here with a granddaughter, Mrs Willson, a young Grenadier officer's lethargic wife, and her baby; also Mrs Willson's sister, Julie, aged 16, very bright and well informed. On my arrival they conducted me around the outside of the house, and after tea round the inside. In the church is a monument which Adam designed for a Curzon, with background pyramid. It is dull and uninspired. Lord Curzon's own monument to himself and his first wife is splendid. His marble effigy was put in place during his lifetime.

Structurally the house is fairly sound, but superficially tattered – the dust sheets don't look as though put on by a trained housemaid – and minor dilapidations are evident. The bluejohn inlay of the Music Room chimneypiece is flaking off. I think only Syon [Park] can be compared to Kedleston for splendour. Americans have unscrewed and stolen the centre of the door handles for souvenirs, the brutes.

KNOLE, *Kent*
(1946)

The largest 'olden tyme' mansion in England, seat of the Sack-villes for four centuries, Knole was well known to J.L.-M., who had often stayed there with his friend Eddy Sackville-West, Lord Sackville's son and heir. Its donation to the National Trust involved years of discussions to overcome legal problems.

18 *March 1943*
At 2 o'clock to Martin's Bank at which were present Colonel Robin Buxton, Lord Sackville, his solicitor, and Lord Willingdon [trustees of the Knole estate with whom J.L.-M. was to discuss its donation]. They had been lunching well, and I was given a glass of port. Lord Sackville could not have been more friendly or anxious to co-operate. I can't think why Eddy does not like him more. He is gentle and sympathetic and always treats me with paternal affection because I am a friend of Eddy. We left it that I was to send him Garrard the estate agent's figures for his comments, whereafter the trustees would decide how much endowment they could and would provide – the capital suggested is enough to yield £3,000 p.a. I am not sure how pleased the Trust will be with me for disclosing these figures, but I believe we must always be absolutely frank with decent donors like Lord Sackville. My sympathies are always with them. In

fact my loyalties are first to the houses, second to the donors, and third to the National Trust. I put the Trust last because it is neither a work of art nor a human being but an abstract thing, a convenience.

5 September 1946

To Knole. Lord Sackville sits there, very thin, almost tiny, gaunt about the nose and with very gleaming false teeth which he picks, like Eddy. He laughs inwardly, without comment and as though in agreement with us, when we assure him that the NT will do nothing without his prior sanction. Mason [Lord Sackville's agent] is always deferential to 'his lordship', and abounding in humour and common sense. Going round the rooms this morning I was horrified by piles of dust under the chairs from worm borings. The gesso furniture is also in a terrible state. All the picture labels want renewing; the silver cleaning; the window mullions mending.

7 October 1946

To Knole again with Ralph Edwards to complete his valuation. An awful old scarecrow accompanied us, called Fletcher the craftsman, looking like an undertaker. When we met Lord Sackville he dropped a great brick by saying, 'The condition of the furniture is deplorable, caused by utter neglect', at which Lord S. bridled. We tried desperately to pick the brick up. For the first time I went into the barracks, or attics, miles of long galleries, with remains of plaster ceilings and some fine Jacobean chimneypieces, under the roofs. Here the visiting retainers used to sleep.

20 May 1947

I agreed with Mason to raise the wages of the Knole staff who are a little dissatisfied that they received so few tips because of the large crowds. Saw Lord Sackville who wants the NT to take the North Wing off his shoulders. The public amuse themselves by carving their names on the oak door of the gatehouse on days when they are not admitted to the state rooms.

LACOCK ABBEY, *Wiltshire*
(1944)

A wonderful survival, much of it consisting of medieval ecclesi-astical buildings, Lacock was presented to the Trust by Miss Matilda Talbot, granddaughter of the pioneer photographer William Fox Talbot who had made his discoveries there.

15 December 1943

I reached Lacock Abbey at 2. Miss Talbot was bustling about the great Sanderson Millar [eighteenth-century architect] hall as I entered. A large log fire was burning, and the room was filled with smoke which blackened the walls and ceiling. It was warm and smelled sweet and cosy. Miss Talbot said, 'I hate fresh air. It is the cause of most of our ills in England.' She is a dear, selfless woman, and extremely high-minded. She has the most unbending sense of duty towards her tenants and estate to the extent that she allows herself only a few hundreds a year on which to live. She spends hardly a farthing on herself, and lives like an anchorite. She wants to hand over Lacock now, abbey and village.

LAMB HOUSE, *Rye, Sussex*
(1948)

The American novelist Henry James lived and worked in this house in his later years.

17 August 1948

On to Rye where we found Mrs Henry James [widow of the novelist's nephew], her niece and solicitor at the Mermaid Inn. Walked round to Lamb House, which she offers with the garden to the National Trust. A delightful George I house in a narrow back street, on a corner. A great tragedy is the complete destruction of the garden house where Henry James wrote from 1898 to 1916. It was a simple structure judging from photographs and I would have it rebuilt. E. F. Benson rented Lamb House after Henry James's death, until he died in 1941 or thereabouts. All the windows remain blown out. Hardboard has been temporarily substituted, so the rooms are pitch dark. They are nearly all panelled. The stair balusters are twisted and the treads shallow and broad, beautiful to walk up and down. The house is in bad condition but can be repaired easily. It is fully furnished with much furniture that belonged to the novelist. His pictures still hanging on the walls. Mrs James told me that the most intimate belongings, including writing-table and piano, were destroyed with the garden house. Much of the rest was removed to America by the family on the novelist's death. She is unable to 'give' what furniture remains in the house, but we have the option to buy it. So Robin [Fedden, NT official] is going to pick out what he thinks ought to remain, with the assistance of Henry James's old secretary who is still alive.

LINDISFARNE CASTLE, *Northumberland* (1944)

Romantically situated on Holy Island, this pile had been transformed into a luxurious Edwardian residence by Lutyens for Edward Hudson, owner of Country Life, *and was later bought by the city financier Edward de Stein, who presented it to the Trust.*

15 September 1945

From Berwick I was driven to Beale foreshore, where I changed into a ramshackle, rusty old car which drove me in the dark across the sands to Holy Island, quite three miles away. Although the tide was out we splashed through water on parts of the causeway, for the sands are never thoroughly dry. Sometimes a horse and cart have to be used, and when the tide is up, a motor boat. There are two lines of posts to guide vehicles, for off the track the sands are treacherous. A weird, open, grey expanse of mudflat with millions of worm-casts, flights of duck over one's head, and pencilled hills in the distance. The car mounts the bank of the island shore, and bumbles along a tolerable road through the little village of Lindisfarne. Beyond the village is Lindisfarne Castle, perched high up on an abrupt rock. The car bumps over the grass and stops. Mr de Stein and a friend were there to greet me. We walked up a cobbled path to the portcullis, and then further steps. A family of islanders looks after the Castle, and serves de Stein whenever he comes here.

De Stein is a peppery, fussy, schoolmasterish man, with whom I should hate to have a row. He has not got a good manner. After dinner we had a talk about mysticism. He recommended a book by William James on the subject. The friend staying is about my age, fair-haired, stocky, an expert botanist who has worked in East Africa, attached in some way to Kew Gardens, and now in the army. Rather nice. I can't quite make de Stein out. He is prudish and disapproving, yet he puts his arm round one's waist and makes rapid, sly remarks which I think it best to leave unheeded.

LITTLE MORETON HALL, *Cheshire*
(1938)

This picture-postcard black-and-white manor house had been admired by Jim's parents, as a result of which he had come to hate it as a boy; but he later did his best to save it through the National Trust.

27 April 1945
From Mow Cop station I climbed the steep hill to the ridiculous castle folly which belongs to the N. Trust. It

blew so hard at the top that I could scarcely breathe. Having inspected this monument associated with the Primitive Methodists, I descended across the fields to Little Moreton Hall. A truly picturesque scene, with the cows lying – it is going to rain – before the moat. The house looked more grotesque than ever; the gallery is so uneven and undulating that it must topple over into the moat. The chapel end subsides in an acute angle. And yet it stands like the Tower of Pisa. How, I wonder? I love the old-fashioned farmyard atmosphere, the heavy, polished Victorian furniture in the great hall, the brown teapot, the scones and marmalade and eggs for luncheon. Charming farmeresses waiting on me, and gossiping with each other, and for ever polishing.

LYME PARK, *Cheshire*
(1946)

This great Elizabethan house, 'Italianized' in the eighteenth century, was accepted by the National Trust in order to be leased to and managed by Stockport Council.

25 November 1943

I caught the 10.15 for Stockport, where I was met and driven to Lyme Park. As we climbed the long drive there was snow lying on the ground. This vast seat is 800 feet above sea level. The park gates are at the entrance to the suburbs of Stockport. In other words Lyme forms a bulwark against Manchester and its satellite horrors. The greater part of the 3,000-acre property stretches in the opposite direction, towards the Peak. All morning while I was in the train the sun was shining. At Lyme it was snowing from a leaden sky. A butler met me at the front door and conducted me through the central courtyard, up some stone steps and into the hall on the piano nobile. Lord Newton lives and eats in the great library with a huge fire burning, and two equally huge dogs lying at his feet.

Lyme is one of England's greatest houses. The exterior is practically all Leoni's work. The south side is a little too severe to be beautiful. Lewis Wyatt's chunky, square tower over the pediment is ponderous, like the central imposition on Buckingham Palace. A corridor runs the whole way round the first floor (from which state rooms open), with windows looking into the courtyard (which is architecturally the most satisfying composition at Lyme). The contents of the state rooms are magnificent, notably the Chippendale chairs, the Charles II beds and the Mortlake tapestries. There is a fascinating Byronic portrait of Thomas Legh in Greek costume standing by a horse. My bedroom on the west side of the first floor has two Sargent portraits, one of Lord Newton's mother and the other of his mother-in-law.

Lord Newton is hopeless. The world is too much for him, and no wonder. He does not know what he can do, ought to do or wants to do. He just throws up his hands in despair. The only thing he is sure about is that his descendants will never want to live at Lyme after an unbroken residence of 600 years. I am already sure that he will not see out his ownership.

There were forty evacuated children in the house,

but they have now gone. The park is cut to pieces by thousands of RAF lorries, for it is at present a lorry depot.

23 December 1943
I lunched with Lord and Lady Newton at their flat in Park Street. They were pleased with the suggestion that Manchester University might rent Lyme Park from the Trust. Lady Newton must once have been handsome. She is tall, and thin like everyone else these days. But she is as languid and hopeless as her husband. Both said they would never be able to reconcile themselves to the new order after the war. They admitted that their day was done, and life as they had known it was gone for ever. How right they are, poor people.

MOSELEY OLD HALL, *Staffordshire*

When Jim visited this property, its proud recent purchaser merely agreed to grant restrictive covenants to the National Trust to prevent its future development; but it was eventually donated to the Trust.

12 May 1944
At 2 I reached Bloxwich, a suburb of Walsall, and went to the offices of Messers Wiggin & Co. Old Mr Wiggin received me and told me he was chairman of a family business of stainless steel, founded by his father. He was immensely proud of it. Showed me brochures of hideously designed coffee pots, thermos flasks, etc. A

fortnight ago he bought Moseley Old Hall from the colliery company which has owned it, and is touchingly pleased. His life's ambition has been to own this house. He does not want to live in it, or to make it a show place, but to restore it with the best expert advice, keep it as a place to take the firm's distinguished guests to, and, in short, to gloat over it. I suggested covenants with the National Trust. He was delighted with the idea. One by one he summoned his two sons and two brothers, to each of whom in turn I had to explain the meaning of covenants. The old man was slow of speech. He appealed to his family to approve his motives and intentions point by point, delivering himself of an inspired sermon. He reminded me of some Old Testament prophet addressing a tribe. It was a curious party and I was struck by the earnestness and sincerity and public spirit of this very worthy family, clustered around the revered autocrat, the patriarch. Then a brother and a son motored me to Moseley. To my pleasant surprise the old Hall is still in remote country, surrounded by and approached through lanes. Unhappily there are several fields of colliery pit heads and pylons in the near distance. The curious purple brick case stuck on to the outside in the 1870s is rather appealing. Of course I should prefer to see the half-timbering revealed, if it were possible, which I doubt. The Hall is a farmhouse, which is nice. The interior has scarcely altered since Charles II took refuge in it after the Battle of Worcester [1651]. It is a pity that the secret hides have lost their secrecy, their door slides have become hinged and handled. But they survive. The attic chapel, Father Huddleston's chamber, the King's little square black hole in which he crouched, are intact. The place is redolent of papistry, monarchy and sanctity.

NOSTELL PRIORY, *Yorkshire*
(1950s)

Seat of Lord St Oswald (whose ancestor had built it on the site of the medieval priory dedicated to that saint), noted for its fine classical interiors by Robert Adam and James Paine.

20 October 1946

We went to tea at Nostell Priory, the Winns. Charles Winn is the present owner, his father having disinherited the elder son, now Lord St Oswald. Winn aged about forty-five, bluff, exquisite manners in that English natural way, unlike the Frogs. It was foggy as we approached. The Paine block is too squat for its length and the Adam addition is not in scale or in proportion. We spent one-and-a-half hours looking over the inside and even then did not get as far as the Adam block, where I understand the decoration to be nineteenth century. In the Paine block the Adam hall is superb and the Adam drawing-room a restrained variant of the music room at Home House [Portman Square, London]. All these rooms still under dust-sheets and the furniture piled in heaps. Could not therefore see the famous Chippendale things. The outside of the house is pitch black, there being a mine only 100 yards from the house. The park large and not very beautiful. Lord and Lady Strathallan staying, both very handsome. Mrs Winn, the third wife, appeared at tea, a friendly, pretty American. Paine's few rooms likewise fine, and distinctly rococo. This house, like Wentworth [Woodhouse], has a number of lovely eighteenth-century wallpapers. Nothing is shabby and the place is well kept up for the Winns are rich. During the war they put away everything for safety, and all the pictures were taken out of the beautiful inset frames.

OSTERLEY, *Middlesex*
(1949)

This Adam masterpiece just outside London was owned by Jim's friend Lord ('Grandy') Jersey, who had entertained him there before the war. As with Knole, years of complicated negotiations took place before the house and park were transferred to the National Trust, who gave them to be managed by the Victoria & Albert Museum.

29 March 1944
What a decline since 1939! Now total disorder and disarray. Bombs have fallen in the park, blowing out many windows; the Adam orangery has been burnt out, and the garden beds are totally overgrown. We did not go round the house which has been taken over by Glyn Mills bank, but round the confines of the estate. There are still 600 acres as yet unsold. Smith [Hubert Smith, NT agent] and I both deprecated the breezy way in which the Osterley agent advocated further slices to the south-east of the house being sold for building development, in order to raise an endowment.

2 March 1947

Grandy Jersey was at Osterley to receive us and conduct us round the house. The visitors were greatly impressed by the quality of Adam's decoration. The state rooms are more or less arranged again and in fairly good repair, but the window frames are all deteriorating. The outside is horribly untidy owing to the brick huts built up to the house by Glyn's Bank, which still occupies most of it.

28 October 1948

At Osterley this morning I walked round the garden for the first time in ages. Behind the cedars to the west of the house is a circuit of trees. It is sad to think what the place is bound to become when made over to the public. The temples are all dilapidated, beds overgrown. Before the war they were immaculate, perhaps too much so.

16 November 1949

In the afternoon I went to Osterley. Was conducted to a turret room and presented with a key on which there was a large label addressed to me. A cupboard was sealed with my name on it. All this was done by Grandy Jersey. Inside the cupboard was a mass of bills and accounts of the Child family in the eighteenth century concerning the building of the house and the making of the furniture. Presumably G. has some good reason for wanting me to look through them before any of the V&A officials.

OWLETTS, *Kent*
(1938)

A Charles II house, home of the architect Sir Herbert Baker.

27 November 1942

To Owletts. Sir Herbert Baker, who has had a stroke, is eighty, kind, Christian-like and cultivated. He was reading French poetry when I arrived. He insists on accompanying one, dragging his legs in a manner which pains one as it must pain him. We lunched and discussed which pieces of furniture [designed by himself] ought to stay permanently in the house. Lady Baker is no less delightful. She was an Edmeades of Nurstead Court, two miles away. They call themselves, with justifiable pride, yeomen of Kent. The Bakers have lived at Owletts since 1780. Both are of stalwart stock, integrity written in their faces. Lady Baker said to her husband, 'I wonder if future generations will attribute all decent buildings of these times to Lutyens or Baker?' I feel that in spite of his detractors – and he is not popular today – there is something great about him when he is being creative and not merely imitative.

PACKWOOD HOUSE, *Warwickshire*
(1941)

*Donated to the National Trust during the war by the Birming-
ham industrialist Graham Baron Ash, whose father had
bought and restored it.*

5 January 1947
Then to Packwood and lunched with Baron. We had
sherry and *pâté de foie gras*, as good as it used to be;
omelette with quince jam and rum blazing; port wine.
Baron conducted me over the house which is now in
pristine condition. He showed me a Victorian lithograph
of the house looking much as it does today. Saw the
servants' wing adapted for the caretaker, and discussed
this. B. wants a disabled ex-officer, not an artistic person.
We don't see eye-to-eye over this.

PETWORTH, *Sussex*
(1947)

*Lord Leconfield was at first hostile to the National Trust, but
Jim eventually won him round to donating his property.*

19 July 1945
I arrived at Petworth at 3.30. I stopped at the street entrance, walked through a long, gloomy passage, crossed
a drive, passed under a *porte cochère* into a hall, and was
ushered into Lord Leconfield's presence. He gave me a

hurried handshake without a smile, and told the house-keeper to show me round inside. This she did, bewailing the damage caused to ceilings and walls by Saturday's storm. She and one housemaid look after this vast palace. All the state rooms being shut up and the furniture under dust-sheets, I had difficulty, with most of the shutters fastened, in seeing. I liked the housekeeper. She keeps the house spotless and polished. Then I was handed back to Lord Leconfield.

My first impression was of a pompous old ass, with a blue face and fish eyes. He seemed deliberately to misunderstand what the National Trust was all about. He was highly suspicious. He looked up and said, 'Understand, this visit commits me to nothing. I much doubt whether the National Trust can help me.' He complained, understandably enough, of surtax, and would not grasp that the Trust was exempt from taxation. He implied that we would turn him out of the house the moment we took over. He walked me very slowly round the park. He said that the Victorian architect Salvin, when summoned by his father, stood on a mound in the park, and pointing to the house, said, 'My Lord, there is only one thing to be done. Pull the whole house down and rebuild it.' His father replied, 'You had better see the inside first.'

At 5.45 Lord Leconfield, tired out, led me to the street door where he dismissed me. Pointing to a tea house with an enormous notice CLOSED hanging in the window, he said, 'You will get a very good tea in there. Put it down to me. Goodbye.'

3 February 1947

Caught the 11.18 to Pulborough where I was met and driven through slush and snow to Petworth. Lord Leconfield, now indeed slow, old and blue-faced, waddled to meet me, clad in yellow gaiters and followed by a black retriever who seems to be his only friend. He is a pathetic old man. Today he was very friendly and not at all pompous or absurd. Wished me to see all the furniture, and hoped I would be pleased with its condition. Said in fact he was convinced he was wise in handing over to the NT. We lunched together, I not sent to the servants' hall. Promptly at 1.30 he summoned the nice old housekeeper to take me round the house. Furniture in splendid condition, smelling of mansion polish and camphor. Lord Leconfield joined us upstairs and waddled around. He is sweet with the servants, they curiously subservient and sycophantic. He made me walk in the cold, steely hail outside. I don't believe he was aware of it. The back of the house, with its buttresses, is really very ugly. I left by bus for Pulborough at four, Lord L. accompanying me to bus stop.

POLESDEN LACEY, *Surrey*
(1942)

A Georgian house restored as a luxurious Edwardian residence, Polesden was left to the National Trust along with most of her huge fortune by the society hostess Mrs Ronnie Greville on her death in 1942.

9 October 1942

At 2.30 I attended a meeting of Mrs Ronnie Greville's executors. A most interesting and complex subject, involving an estate of some £2 million. Mrs Greville has left Marie Antoinette's necklace to the Queen, £20,000 to Princess Margaret Rose and £25,000 to the Queen of Spain. Everyone in London is agog to hear the terms of Mrs G.'s will. She was a lady who loved the great because they were great, and apparently had a tongue dipped in gall. I remember old Lady Leslie exclaiming, 'Maggie Greville! I would sooner have an open sewer in my drawing-room.'

14 October 1942

I motored with Captain Hill to Polesden Lacey. The house was built by Cubitt in 1818 and looks from a distance across the valley much as it did in Neale's view of that date. The interior was, I imagine, entirely refitted by Mrs Greville, in the expensive taste of an Edwardian millionairess. But it is not vulgar. It is fitted with good things, and several museum pieces. The upstairs rooms are well appointed, in six or seven self-contained suites with bathrooms attached. There is a grass courtyard in the middle of the house.

Mrs Greville has been buried in the rose garden to the west of the house, next to the dog cemetery in accordance with female country house owner tradition. The gardens are unostentatious and rather beautiful: the grounds very beautiful, with a splendid view across the vale from the south front to the wooded hill beyond. Queen Mary's Walk is a straight grass ride bordered with yew.

25 November 1942
Harold [Nicolson] talked of Mrs Greville, a common, waspish woman who got where she did through persistence and money. She was her father's illegitimate child, her mother being unknown. She married reputable, dull Captain Ronnie Greville, and jumped off from this safe spring-board. She build herself a fictitious reputation for cleverness, and was not even witty. But she had the ambition to cultivate ambassadors and entertain them at Polesden Lacey, so that in her constant travels she could demand return favours in special trains and red carpets, to the chagrin of foreign officials.

SALTRAM PARK, *Devon*
(1957)

Like Nostell, a mansion remarkable for its opulent Robert Adam interiors.

6 August 1953
Lord Morley succeeded his brother at Saltram [Park, Devon] a year ago. He is 73, permanently drunk, has had to pay enormous death duties, has no children, yet has nobly spent over £10,000, his agent informed us, in decorating the state rooms from top to bottom. It is very well done by Keebles [the decorators], and one of the

best Adam interiors I have seen. Lord Morley was away but in the saloon was his butler, wearing his lordship's Brigade uniform, the earl's coronet and coronation robes at his elbow, sitting to a pretty American female artist.

SHERBORNE CASTLE, *Dorset*
(1980s)

Another house whose blimpish owners, though they did not like the National Trust, eventually bequeathed their property to it.

28 January 1944

At 10 the solicitor took me to Rawlence the agent's office, and the three of us motored to the castle grounds bordering the town. At first glance the outside of the house is disappointing. The cement rendering makes it gloomy. The plate-glass windows give it a blind, eyeless look. Yet the house reminds me of Westwood Park [Worcestershire] in that it too has a central Elizabethan block (built as a hunting lodge by Sir Walter Raleigh) to which four arms were added in Restoration times. The dressings are of Ham stone. Fine entrance gates at the north and south sides, forming two open courts. Like Westwood the house is terribly confusing inside, for it is very tall, with many floor levels. There is little inside to take the breath away, but much that is good, notably the great marble chimneypieces of Jacobean date and, above all, the two interior porches in the downstairs dining-room. At present the furniture is stored away, for American troops have requisitioned the castle.

So far the lordly owner has not appeared, and we three of low degree lunch at the hotel. Twice Rawlence is called away to be advised by the Colonel's butler at what time we are to appear for coffee, port and cigars. The Wingfield Digbys are in Raleigh's lodge for 'the duration'. The Colonel is a stooping MFH with the manner of one. Very autocratic, and conscious of his not inconsiderable dignity. He addresses Rawlence as Major Rawlence, in spite of the latter's father and grandfather also having been agents to the family, and Rawlence being every inch a gent. Rawlence addresses him as Colonel, and often as Sir. An awkward interview takes place. I explain as best I can what the transaction would involve. But they are not the sort of people to welcome public access.

After the interview we sallied forth to the pleasance. The Colonel and Mrs W.D. took us over the old ruined castle and through the very beautiful wooded walks by the lake. Here we came upon Raleigh's seat, where the servant is said to have thrown the water over his master while he was smoking, and Pope's seat, where the poet wrote letters to Martha Blount. The Colonel showed little interest in these fascinating associations. 'Pope indeed,' he snorted. 'I've no idea which pope it could have been.'

The Wingfield Digbys, finding that I was to dine alone, very kindly bade me dine with them. They showed me some rare miniatures; also a jewel given to Ambassador Digby by the court of Spain. I liked the W.D.s, although aware that they might not like me. And there was one awkward moment when, à propos of nothing, the Colonel exclaimed, 'I can't stick Roman Catholics. One can smell 'em a mile off', or words to that effect. Mrs Wingfield Digby, who, although her sentiments were clearly the same as her husband's, wished to appear open-minded, then said, 'But, Freddy, they do have a right to their own point of view', adding after a pregnant pause, 'Of course, one can't trust them one yard.' I [J.L.-M. was a Catholic convert] thought it best to remain mum.

SISSINGHURST, *Kent*
(1967)

Owned by the writer and poet Vita Sackville-West, who created a famous garden there with her husband Harold Nicolson. An intimate friend of both Vita and Harold and a frequent visitor to the house, Jim helped get the property accepted by the National Trust when her son Nigel offered it after her death in 1962.

29 June 1949

Motored to Sissinghurst to stay the night with Vita. The garden here is almost blowsy with bloom. Surely no other county but Kent can be so lush and rich. I asked Vita why she liked the old-fashioned roses so much. She said because they reminded her of the Tudor heraldic roses and Caroline stump-work. The Sissinghurst garden enchants because it is both formal and informal. The straight paths lined with yew and the pleached lime alleys lead to orchards, their fruit trees swathed in ramblers and eglantines.

She and I sat down to dinner at 8 o'clock. A cold meal with white wine which we drank and drank until 12.20 when we left the table. Vita is adorable. I love her romantic disposition, her southern lethargy concealing unfathomable passions, her slow movements of grave dignity, her fund of human kindness, understanding and desire to disentangle other people's perplexities for them. I love her deep plum voice and chortle. We talked of love and religion. She told me that she learnt only at twenty-five that her tastes were homosexual. It was sad that homosexual lovers were considered by the world to be slightly comical. The memory of this evening will be ineradicable.

SMALLHYTHE PLACE, *Kent*
(1938)

A museum to the memory of the actress Ellen Terry who had lived there, now inhabited by her daughter Edith Craig and her lesbian coterie.

26 March 1942
Left for Smallhythe. Miss Edith Craig was in bed, but the two other odd old ladies were about, Christopher St John and Tony (really Clare) Atwood. They were dressed in corduroy trousers and men's jackets, one homespun, the other curry tweed. Their grey locks were

hacked short and both wore tam-o'shanters. They were charming to me and gave me a huge two-handled mug of coffee. In Ellen Terry's little house one feels that she might walk past one at any minute, and in her bedroom that she might appear sitting before her dressing-table brushing her hair.

Edith Craig died in March 1947, just a few weeks after her mother's centenary had been celebrated with a service at St Paul's, Covent Garden.

15 April 1947

I drove down to Kent, singing all the way as loudly as I could, unheard. Passed Knole and lunched at Tenterden. At 2 o'clock called at Smallhythe. The two poor old women remaining were very pathetic. Miss Atwood, aged eighty-two, is the more spry and affable. Miss St John, very lame, was wearing brown corduroy trousers, stretched tight over an enormous bum, a yellow scarf around her neck, a magenta beret on her grey hair, shirt and tie. The other one wore a shirt and tie too and is called Tony by her friends; Miss St J. is called Chris. They showed me over the property and explained its problems. In the Ferry Cottage lives a terrifying woman who helps them with the housework. She wears grey flannel trousers, tight shirt and tie and beret, and is grubby and masculine. She is called Bruce, and refers to Miss St John as 'Mr Chris'. Really I felt like Alice in Wonderland.

STOURHEAD, *Wiltshire*
(1947)

Sir Henry Hoare, of the banking family, whose only son had been killed in the First World War, offered to bequeath this house with its splendid park to the National Trust together with an endowment of £100,000.

12 October 1942

By appointment with Sir Henry Hoare, I was at the County Hotel, Salisbury, by 2 o'clock. I gave my name to the porter and sat in the dreary lounge to wait. A young RAF sergeant came in and sat down. I looked up and saw a face of ineffable beauty which smiled in a most beseeching manner. The sergeant took out a cigarette, offered me one, and was about to introduce himself when, damn it!, Sir Henry Hoare was announced.

Sir Henry is an astonishing nineteenth-century John Bull, hobbling on two sticks. He was wearing a pepper and salt suit and a frayed grey billycock over his purple face. He had a very bronchial cough and kept hoiking and spitting into an enormous carrot-coloured handkerchief. He talked about his bad knee, and told me he had lost a knee-cap. I found myself shouting, for he is rather deaf, 'Do you find it much of a handicap having no knee-cap?' After the third repetition I decided that my question was inept.

Lady Hoare is an absolute treasure, and unique. She is tall, ugly and eighty-two; dressed in a long black skirt, belled from a warp waist and trailing over her ankles.

She has a thick net blouse over a rigidly upholstered bosom, complete with stiff, whaleboned high collar round the throat. Over this a black and white check jacket, evidently reinforced with stays, for it ends in tight points over her thighs. The sleeves are exaggeratedly mutton-chop. She has a protruding square coif of frizzly grey hair in the style of the late nineties, black eyebrows and the thickest spectacle lenses I have ever seen. She adores the memory of George Lloyd [Lord Lloyd of Dolobran (1879–1941), imperial proconsul whom J.L.-M. had served as private secretary, 1932–5] and is quite convinced that he was the greatest Englishman of this century.

The Hoares took me round the house, which is packed to the brim with good things like cheap bamboo cake stands and thin silver vases filled with peacock feathers. On the grand piano an impenetrable forest of silver photograph frames. The house was gutted by fire in 1902 and rebuilt by Sir Aston Webb from old photographs and records. There are some rococo chimneypieces brought after the fire from another Hoare house in Northamptonshire. Only the Regency picture gallery and library in the projecting wings were spared. All the contents however were saved, including the wonderful suite of furniture by the younger Chippendale.

For dinner we had soup, whiting, pheasant, apple pie, dessert, a white Rhine wine and port. Lady Hoare has no housemaid, only a cook and butler. But she said with satisfaction, 'The Duchess of Somerset at Maiden Bradley has to do all her own cooking.' She kept up a lively, not entirely coherent prattle. She said to me, 'Don't you find the food better in this war than in the last?' I replied that I was rather young during the last war, but I certainly remembered the rancid margarine we were given at my preparatory school when I was eight. 'Oh!' she said. 'You were lucky. We were reduced to eating rats.' I was a little surprised, until Sir Henry looked up and said, 'No, no, Alda. You keep getting your wars wrong. That was when you were in Paris during the Commune.'

The National Trust inherited the house, together with its park and entire contents, when the Hoares died on the same day in March 1947.

21 May 1947

We reached Stourhead at 3 o'clock. By that time the sun had penetrated the mist, and was gauzy and humid. The air about the lake and grounds of a conservatory consistency. Never do I remember such Claude-like, idyllic beauty here. See Stourhead and die. Rhododendrons and azaleas full out. No ponticums, but pink and deep red rhododendrons – not so good – and loveliest of all, the virginal snow white ones, almost too good to be true. Azaleas mostly orange and brimstone. These clothe the banks of the lake. The beech are at their best. We walked leisurely round the lake and amused ourselves in the grot trying to remember Pope's four lines correctly by heart, and forgetting, and running back to memorize. The temples are not in bad order, the Temple of Flora and the Pantheon being particularly well kept. We had tea at the inn at Stourton; then walked rapidly round the first floor of the house. We were staggered by the amount of first-rate furniture and pictures. There is more than enough upstairs to fill the whole *piano nobile*.

TEMPLE SOWERBY MANOR, *Westmorland* (*now known as* ACORN BANK)

26 May 1943

I spent all day yesterday in the train from Euston to Windermere. This morning Bruce Thompson [NT representative in Lake District] motored me through heavy rain across the moors, to Kendal and Appleby. The intermittent sun and great plumes of black smoke made a sublime scene, sweeping and chasing each other across the moors. Yet, cockney that I have become, I find the mountains lonely and depressing. We moved on to Temple Sowerby, the McGrigor-Philips house. Mrs McGrigor-Philips is a tall, ungainly, exceedingly coy woman, and a low-brow writer [now valued for her poetry in Yorkshire dialect] under the pen-name of Dorothy Una Ratcliffe. He is a grubby, red-visaged, hirsute old teddy bear. They laid down a lot of nonsensical conditions in making over the house, intending to provide the minimum endowment although she is a millionairess, having inherited a fortune from her uncle, Lord Brotherton [in fact the uncle of her first husband, Charles Ratcliffe]. Bruce Thompson was infinitely patient and polite, and only occasionally betrayed what he was thinking by pursing his lips. The house, which I once saw in 1938, is of tawny orange sandstone. Although the core of the house is Jacobean, what one now sees is eighteenth century. Temple Sowerby is at present occupied by the Railway Wagon Repairers and their families. The Philipses retain one small wing and a caravan for a bedroom. The walk above the flowering burn at the rear of the house is very romantic. From the front are distant views across green pastures of the mountains in the Lake District. It is a lovely setting.

11 August 1943
Bruce Thompson is in a great state because he left behind at Temple Sowerby during our visit his file containing letters between him and me, criticizing Mrs McGrigor-Philips. Some of mine were strongly worded and I remember saying she was an impossible woman to do business with. Mrs McGrigor-Philips read all the correspondence and has written to the secretary and the chairman complaining of our misconduct. She said to Bruce on the telephone, 'I thought you were both gentlemen', which upset Bruce who is 100 per cent a gentleman to my 25 per cent. I told him he ought to have retorted, 'And I thought you were a lady.' For ladies do not read other people's letters.

UPPARK, *Sussex*
(1950s)

Like the Massingberds at Gunby, the Meade-Fetherstonhaughs, owners of this romantic house in the Sussex Downs, were prepared to sacrifice everything they had to ensure its survival in the National Trust's hands.

12 January 1946

Motored in the office Morris to Uppark in Sussex. Lady Meade-Fetherstonhaugh kindly gave me coffee – stone cold – from a pot she held over a log fire. She was welcoming and friendly and most anxious that our scheme should succeed. The country round here is heavenly, rolling downs under a pellucid sea-light. Backed by a belt of trees the house commands a panoramic view of sheep-cropped sward and the sea. A romantic house, yet it disappoints me a little. Perhaps because it is so tumbledown, and the slate roof is shiny purple and the elliptical dormers are too spotty. Lady M.-F. showed me all round. She has done wonders repairing the curtains and stuffs and bringing back their old colours by dye from her herb garden. Saponaria is her great secret. She is a first-rate needlewoman and, before the war interrupted her work, spent years labouring away. During the war she had to do her own housework and so the fabric repairs were neglected. She showed me one curtain which was a heap of dull silk tatters, and another, which she has retrieved from a like state. It is a deep, live mulberry colour, minutely hemmed and stitched. The contents of the house are marvellous. She told me that Eddie [Earl] Winterton was ruled out of inheritance by old Miss Fetherstonhaugh before she died in 1895. He was brought there as a child by his mother and was rather rude; asked his mother why Miss F. dropped her h's, and if he was to own the place one day. The Lady Leconfield of the day was ruled out too. Miss F. asked her what she would do with the silver, if the place was left to her. 'Take it to Petworth of course,' she said.

There are no servants in the house now at all. Lady M.-F. and the Admiral gave us luncheon and tea in the basement. Their lives are completely and utterly sacrificed to the house, and they and their son love it. Mr Cook's agent, Hill [Ernest Cook of the travel agency dynasty was a rich philanthropist who bought several houses for the National Trust], is determined they shall part with all the contents for the inclusive offer of £50,000, with which sum they have to endow the house. So they, poor things, will get nothing in cash out of the transaction.

UPTON HOUSE, *Warwickshire*
(1947)

Lord Bearsted, like Lord Fairhaven the son of an oil tycoon, wished to donate his house together with its great collection and a handsome endowment.

1–2 March 1946
I reached Upton at 6.30 to stay with the Bearsteds. He and Lady B. both charming, with the unassuming manners of the well-bred. At midnight Lord B. took me round the house. Inside there is nothing of consequence architecturally save a few early eighteenth-century chimneypieces and a beautiful Coleshill-style staircase, rearranged by Lord B. and extended. Morley Horder, the architect, built on to the house in the 1920s. But heavens, the contents! There is a lot of Chippendale-style furniture and some marvellous Chelsea china of the very

best quality. The picture collection superb, as fine as any private collection in England. Many of the pictures are not yet back from the Welsh caves where they were stored with the National Gallery pictures.

[The next morning] walked round the garden with Lord B. and the agent. One side of the house is 1695, the other 1735, but Lord B. has very much enlarged it. The result is pleasing. The grounds are beautiful, a high bank with belt of trees and a steep range of terraces. I am a little doubtful about the propriety of accepting this place, and without contents the offer could not be entertained.

5 November 1946

Staying with the Bearsteds. More of his pictures are back from war storage, including the Italian primitives. The whole make a superb private collection. An undergraduate from Oxford, David Carritt [subsequently famous as an art 'detective'], came to look at the pictures. Lord B. warned me beforehand to be kind to him for he would probably be shy. He was by no means shy. A perky youth of eighteen dashed into the room with abounding self-confidence. Within minutes he was disputing the entries in Lord B.'s catalogue. Though polite he was too sure of himself.

THE VYNE, *Hampshire*
(1948)

A large country house which Jim found interesting as it had been lived in for several generations by a family, the Chutes, who were devout evangelicals and remained middle-class in outlook.

18 May 1946
Arrived at 5.45. I liked the Chutes more this time, perhaps because he treated me in a less schoolmasterly, more equal-to-equal manner. It is a beautiful house and the garden looking so green and spruce. The wide lawns all mown again. The school has left and they are living in the whole house because she says you cannot shut up part for the moth and general corruptions. She is a childlike, almost childish woman, but fundamentally sweet. They live in Spartan fashion, and their food is not good. Their views are too conservative and unaccommodating. I slept in the Gothic Room above the tomb chapel. We talked for hours and I think they will hand the place over. They know they must be the last of the family to inhabit the whole house and to submit themselves to its exacting demands. A younger generation which has not lived in it as children could not be expected to do the same. They have no servants living in. Four village ladies come during the week.

18 August 1948

Mr and Mrs Chute received me most kindly, for I had written asking if I might study the Renaissance windows in the Vyne chapel [for J.L.-M.'s book *Tudor Renaissance*]. This I did, and on hands and knees also took notes of the maiolica tiles on the floor in front of the altar. Mr C. kept interrupting me by discussing the terms of his will. People adore reading one extracts from their wills, I notice, breathlessly and without pauses as those idiots, solicitors, draft them without punctuation. I persuaded him to insert a clause whereby the National Trust might control the actual use to which the clergy tenants wish to put particular rooms. Otherwise we shall find abominable bad taste 'bon-dieuserie' disfiguring the Palladian staircase and the early Tudor gallery. Then he showed me a pile of books which he had set aside for sale for, he said, the clergy would not want them. They were Wood's *Palmyra* and other architectural volumes, the sort I would give my eyes for, and I can't think how to persuade him not to part with them. Damn the clergy! For a scholar, Oppidan head of Eton, who spouts Latin tags without cessation, Mr Chute is singularly unimaginative and philistine.

WADDESDON MANOR, *Buckinghamshire* (1957)

The huge endowment which accompanied this Rothschild house would later enable the National Trust to maintain it to a far higher standard than its other houses.

16 May 1946

Trained this morning to Aylesbury and was motored by Mrs James de Rothschild's agent to Waddesdon Manor. What a house! An 1880 pastiche of a François Premier château. Yet it is impressive because it is on the grand scale. There is symmetry, and craftsmanship and finish. I suppose most people today would pronounce it hideous. I find it compelling. A nursery school, which was here throughout the war, has just left. It is being scrubbed and cleaned. The Rothschilds are moving back into the whole of it, which is huge. They have been living in the wing. Most of the rooms are panelled with gilded Louis XV *boiserie*. One drawing-room is lined with marble. Furniture French of the highest quality. One room stacked with pictures, taken out of their frames. A hundred acres of grounds offered too. Beautiful trees. In all a better Cliveden. I have written a report, by no means contemptuous, on it.

WALLINGTON, *Northumberland*
(1941)

Even before its Country Houses Scheme was launched in 1936, the National Trust had been offered this great estate by the radical socialist baronet Sir Charles Treveylan (brother of the historian Professor G. M. Trevelyan who chaired the Trust's Estates Committee). He was a difficult and demanding donor, however, and it was some years before he put his intentions into effect.

25–26 September 1942

I took a bus from Newcastle, standing all the way, and arrived at Wallington at 7.30 in the rain and dark. Matheson [NT Secretary] and John Dower met me by the stables and carried my bag. I was tired and depressed all day, and found the Trevelyan family overpowering in spite of the kind welcome they gave me. Lady Trevelyan came out of the drawing-room in a sweeping, stately rush, shaking my hands warmly and exuding cordiality. When I went into the dining-room Sir Charles rose and shook hands in the same hospitable way. I don't quite know why, because they are dyed-in-the-wool socialists, this should have surprised me. A newly married daughter Patricia, big with child, is living here; so is another daughter Pauline (Mrs Dower). Her husband, the aforementioned John Dower, is working on postwar National Park schemes, is very left-wing, and from his connections and position is, according to Matheson, important.

Lady Trevelyan speaks succinctly, carefully and measuredly, using the north country clipped 'a', and is distinctly 'clever'. Gertrude Bell [the explorer] was her sister. Lady T. is handsome in a 'no nonsense about appearances' manner, and looks as though she may have been the first woman chairman of the L[ondon] C[ounty] C[ouncil]. She is authoritarian, slightly deaf, and wears pince-nez. The two daughters are abrupt and rather terrifying. After dinner I am worn out, and long for bed. But no. We have general knowledge questions. Lady T. puts the questions one after the other with lightning rapidity. I am amazed and impressed by her mental agility, and indeed by that of the daughters, who with pursed lips shoot forth unhesitating answers like a spray of machine-gun bullets. All most alarming to a tired stranger. At the end of the 'game', for that is what they call this preparatory school examination, they allot marks. Every single member of the family gets 100 out of 100. The son-in-law gets 80, Matheson (who is a clever man) gets 30. I get 0. But then I am a half-wit. Deeply humiliated I receive condolences from the Trevelyans and assurances that I shall no doubt do better next time. I make an inward vow that there will never be a next time.

[The next day] I spent morning and afternoon tramping, map in hand, round the entire estate, to Chesters Farm and the distant moorland in the north; and to Scots Gap in the opposite direction. After tea Sir Charles took me round the house. He is seventy-one, rather old and slow, white-haired and bent, with a large nose. He is very like Professor [G. M.] Trevelyan, but less grim. Although an advanced socialist, he has lost his old fanaticism, is courteous, and not absolutely humourless. I quite like him.

The saloon is one of the loveliest rooms I have seen. It has a high coved ceiling, of which the ground colour is the original egg blue, with rococo plaster motifs in white. Under the cornice walls are painted a Naples yellow, verging on terracotta.

WEST WYCOMBE PARK, *Buckinghamshire*
(1943)

On the outbreak of war in 1939, the National Trust offices were evacuated to this Palladian mansion, seat of the Dashwoods and famous for its associations with the Hell-Fire Club. When Jim returned to work there in 1941, three friends – the novelist Nancy Mitford, the music critic Eddy Sackville-West, and Nancy's cousin Clementine Beit – were also staying. The Dashwoods had long been trying to get the house (for which they had little endowment) accepted by the National Trust and the deal was finally done in 1943, shortly after the Trust left to return to London.

1 January 1942

West Wycombe Park is a singularly beautiful eighteenth-century house with one shortcoming. Its principal living-rooms face due north. The south front is overshadowed by a long, double colonnade which induces a total eclipse of the sun from January to December. Consequently we are very cold in the winter, for the radiators work fitfully these days. Our offices are in the Brown Drawing Room and Johnny Dashwood's small study beyond it. Matheson, the Secretary, Miss Paterson [head of the clerical staff], Eardley Knollys [fellow-official] and I work in the latter room; Miss Ballachey, a typist and 'the junior' (aged 15), in the bigger room with all the filing cabinets.

8 February 1942

Yesterday's luncheon revealed Helen [Dashwood, the arrogant chatelaine] in a new light, for the curate and his old mother came. H. said to us just before they arrived that there must be no witticisms and no house-party talk, just the sort of thing Mama would say. They were indeed an eminently 'bedint' couple, and H. said so poor that they undoubtedly didn't have enough to eat. The mother was sadly dressed for the terrible cold, and most humble and pathetic. He a facetious young man in a long black cutaway coat, with black dusty hair badly cut and a blue blotchy face. Yet the two were proud in their reciprocal love. Helen made great efforts to entertain them, and induce them to have a square meal. Alas, they were far too genteel to be pressed to second helpings.

After dinner I took up my knitting – 'the true sock' Clementine calls it, which on St Milne's day, instead of liquefying, will unravel if there is to be a good harvest. Cecil [Beaton] had hiccoughs he laughed so much. Eddy took up his knitting, an endless khaki scarf. We must have looked an odd spectacle. Still, I wish Helen would not call us the two old bombed houses.

1 March 1942

Before luncheon, Nancy said, 'I must just dash to the Beardmore.' 'The what?', Helen asked. 'Don't you know', we said, 'that the upstairs lavatory is called after the Beardmore Glacier. It faces due north, the window is permanently propped open so that it can't be shut, and the floor is under a drift of snow.' Helen doesn't find this a funny joke. After luncheon, Eddy, Nancy and I huddle over a few green logs in the fireplace and turn to discussing H.'s extraordinarily unadult character, her terror of being left out of anything that may be going on, her pique over preconceived plans going wrong, and a certain resentment over others enjoying something she fears she may be missing.

8 April 1942

This afternoon Sarah [Dashwood, daughter of the house] ran into the office at West Wycombe calling for Miss Paterson. The tapestry room chimney was on fire. I dashed upstairs and with Helen went on to the flat roof. Smoke was pouring from the chimney stack. I got a stirrup pump and soaked the stack with water. Within five minutes of the fire being extinguished the fire brigade arrived. I secretly enjoyed the incident. Helen was very scared, which was only natural, looked very white and issued and counter-issued orders in a snappish way.

12 November 1942

Helen has taken the news of our departure manfully. I feel sorry for her, as she will have to look for other lodgers. She knows she may do worse than have us. Yesterday the odious butler walked out of the house at 9.30 without warning because Helen asked him, quite nicely, to fetch her some marmalade for breakfast.

21 August 1943

Caught a morning train to High Wycombe and walked up the drive at West Wycombe just as the Eshers [Lord Esher of the Country Houses Committee and wife] arrived for luncheon with Johnny and Helen [Dash-wood]. Esher was in splendid form, teasing the Dash-woods about their progeny. After luncheon we drove to the far end of the park and inspected the temples, follies and cottages on the property to be transferred; also all that distant part of the park to be held inalienably. Esher has a genius for persuading people to act sensibly against their deep-rooted inclinations by his jocular manner and sheer fun. I really believe we may acquire this beautiful house and park in the end.

23 December 1943
Today the announcement of the National Trust's acquisi-tion of West Wycombe Park appeared in the press: at last, after protracted negotiations since 1938.

WOOLSTHORPE MANOR, *Lincolnshire*
(1943)

The home of Sir Isaac Newton.

5 March 1943
Newton's house in which he was born in 1642 is about twenty years older. It is Cotswoldy, with good steep pitched roof, stone corniced chimneys and mullioned windows. It has four large bedrooms, one of which was partitioned off in about 1666 with panelling of that date so as to form a study for Newton. Upstairs the L-shaped room is said to be the one whence Newton watched the apple fall. The original tree's descendant, now very aged,

stands on the site of its forebear in the little apple orchard in front of the house. The secretary is going to find out what species of apple it is. Tenant farmers have lived for 200 years in the house. The present ones are leaving because all of the surrounding land has been exploited commercially for the limestone, and is now arid, blasted heath and hummocks of infertile slack. It is a scandal that good agricultural land is allowed to be so treated by commercial firms and left thoroughly wasted and useless. The little manor house has light, but no sanitation. There are earth closets in the garden.

PART TWO

Houses Which Escaped the National Trust

ALTHORP, *Northamptonshire*

Seat of the 7th Earl Spencer (grandfather of the future Princess Diana).

5 January 1942

I arrived at Althorp more than half an hour late. Lord Spencer was huffy at first because of my lateness, and because of the depreciation of Althorp by the agent whom the Trust had employed to make a report on the property. He understandably associated the Trust with the agent's ignorance and lack of taste. In the end I liked Lord Spencer for not being crosser than he was. He said I was the first National Trust person who had talked sense. Certainly I appreciated Althorp. But the difficulties will be infinite before we get it. I stayed to luncheon – poached eggs with maize and cabbage – which we ate in a little panelled room. Lady Spencer, like a goddess, distilled charm and gentleness around her.

BREDE PLACE, *Sussex*

24–26 March 1942

I arrived at Brede at 7.30 in time for dinner with Clare Sheridan [sculptress], whom I had not seen for years. She looks a little older, is stout but magnificent. She was wearing corduroy trousers which did not suit her, but the next morning she wore a terracotta skirt with flowing shawl to match. She kept flinging the shawl about her in Isadora Duncan fashion. Clare is a pacifist, and we spoke of the war, and of spiritual values. I found that I agreed with her fundamentally. She is a big woman and has the bigness to remain detached from the war. I remember once thinking that in the event of war most of my friends would have the bigness to remain so detached, but no, none of them seem to be, not even myself. Clare is. It is true that now Dick [her son] is dead, she can afford to be. Clare has woven a spiritual seclusion and wrapped herself in it like a cocoon. She thinks her cousin Winston [Churchill] ought to go. She praises the contrasting virtues of Stafford Cripps, who neither smokes nor drinks, and is impressed by the love of the people in his own village for him.

After breakfast [next day], at which I was offered a goose egg and, like an ass, refused it for fear of appearing greedy, we went down to the park to look at Brede Place, now occupied by soldiers. It is a wonderful house and to my surprise not large. Nothing, save Dick Sheridan's five bathrooms and heating plant, has been added to the house since Henry VIII's reign. A very perfect late medieval house, with a wide view, yet remote. It has several panelled rooms. Clare would sell Brede for £7,000, but there is little land and no other form of endowment. Yet it would let if the Trust held it, I feel sure.

CASTLE BROMWICH HALL, *Warwickshire*

22 September 1945

Lord and Lady Bradford conducted me round Castle Bromwich Hall. It is a fine red-brick house of Elizabethan date with several late seventeenth-century ceilings of the compartmented, bay-wreath type. Much early and much William and Mary panelling. The painted ceiling over the staircase by Laguerre. The house is empty, having been vacated by the troops, and in consequence is a filthy mess. Every window broken by bombs dropped in the garden, all the heraldic glass destroyed in this way. Yet in other respects surprisingly little structural damage incurred. The most alarming threat to the building is the dry-rot which is rampant. The garden, now very neglected, is contained within a brick wall. It has descending terraces, a contemporary maze and holly hedges in the formal style. I would say it is an important and complete garden of *circa* 1700.

Lord Bradford is a very courteous man, the epitome of good breeding. Lady B., whom I like, kept snubbing him. She told him he ought to give the place to the Trust without further thought. What was the good, she said, of letting it to unsatisfactory business firms who had no idea how to look after it? The family would never want to live in it again. This I think is incontrovertible. She pointed out that he had let the stable block to some depot for £100 p.a., out of which he receives, after tax, £2.10s. I suggested that perhaps Birmingham might have some use for this marvellous old house, still so tranquil, so well sited on its hill and yet now so close to the city.

CASTLE HOWARD, *Yorkshire*

2 November 1949

A filthy wet November day. George Howard [the aristo-cratic owner] is stout and uncouth, sometimes forthright to rudeness. Perhaps his heart is kind. How can one tell? Talks a good deal about antiques but is alarmingly ignorant for a National Trust representative and, worse still, without taste. He took me over Castle Howard, now empty, the school having gone. Its aspect is exceedingly forlorn. It is not in bad condition, but very unkempt. It looks sad with the dome and the best rooms burnt out, but there is enough space left for a country house these days, in all conscience. The lack of symmetry in Castle Howard has always worried me. The sculpture of the stonework, cornices, columns, etc., is crisp. George intends to move himself into the East Wing and open the rest to the public. We drove to the Temple of the Four Winds, now in a state of dereliction, but a very elegant building, more Palladian than Baroque. The monopteral, Doric mausoleum is a splendid affair and the bastioned retaining wall forms an impressively massive base. In fact it is a composition of grandeur and genius. We went into the vaults where are many gaping niches unused. George intends to be buried there, the first to be so since the eighteenth century. And so he should be, for he will be the re-creator of Castle Howard. The rotunda chapel above is faultless. The English Georgians were better craftsmen than Palladio's men. George much distressed because hooligans have thrown bricks through the windows, breaking panels of original glass.

CHATSWORTH, *Derbyshire*

J.L.-M. loved this house, the principal seat of the Dukes of Devonshire, and was often to stay there during the last forty years of his life. When he first visited it in 1948, Andrew and Debo Hartington, who two years later succeeded as 11th Duke and his Duchess, were working to open it to the public (though they did not move into it for another ten years). J.L.-M. had known Debo since she was a baby, she being the youngest sister of his Eton schoolfriend Tom Mitford who had been killed in the war.

1–3 August 1948

Debo and Andrew drove me to Chatsworth this morning. The site of the house, the surroundings unsurpassed. The grass emerald green as in Ireland. The Derwent river, although so far below the house, which it reflects, seems to dominate it. Black-and-white cattle in great herds. All the hills have trees along their ridges. Neatness and order are the rule although, Andrew says, there are fourteen gardeners instead of forty before the last war. The inordinate length of the house undeniably impressive, and the 6th Duke's extensions do not make it lopsided, as I had been led to suppose. The limitless landscape can absorb it. The uniform yellow sandstone helps link the old block to Wyatville's towered colonnade, which might be taken out of a Claude painting. We wandered through the gardens, greyhounds streaming across the lawns. Andrew turned on the fountain from the willow tree. Water not only drips from the tree but jets from nozzles all round. The cascade not working this morning, but will be turned on for the public this afternoon. At present the great house is empty, under covers and dust-sheets. Next year the state rooms are to be shown. We entered the house from the west door, let in by Mr Thompson, the librarian. The state rooms are all on the second floor, reminiscent of Hampton Court, one leading to the next without passages. All pictures taken off the walls. Interior terribly hot and stuffy. Andrew let me look through two volumes of Inigo Jones drawings of masque costumes. Henry VII's prayer book, with illuminations, given by the King to his daughter who was asked to pray for him, inscription in his kingly hand.

The scale of Chatsworth is gigantic, beyond comprehension (like St Peter's, Rome) until experienced. The detail of outside stonework of high quality, notably the antlers over windows, frostwork in the central courtyard, the panels of trophies, by Watson presumably. The Tijou ironwork easily identifiable. The Hartingtons, eager to know their possessions, intend to spend several hours a day systematically looking through papers in the library, like schoolchildren at a holiday task. When it comes to working on Inigo Jones, Andrew says I may have full access to the Chatsworth library papers.

As a couple the Hartingtons seem perfection – both

young, handsome, and inspired to accomplish great things. He has a splendid war record and won the MC. Has contested one constituency and is now nursing Chesterfield, a very Socialist seat. Unlikelihood of winning does not deter him. Both full of faith in themselves and their responsibilities. She has all the Mitford virtues and none of the profanity. I admire them very much.

[Next morning] it poured [at Chatsworth], but slackened a bit at eleven. Andrew had to write letters, but Debo and I rode – the first time I have ridden for quite ten years. We went through the great Wyatville entrance and into the gardens of Chatsworth below the terrace. The wooden surrounds of the west front windows are still coloured gold, now rather faint, but the sash-bars have not been gilded that one can see. We went up the hill to look at the Cascade Temple and back again, then across the main road to the far side of the valley to see the Russian Lodge, built by the Bachelor [6th] Duke. His spirit at Chatsworth is very prevalent.

COTHELSTONE HOUSE, *Somerset*

19 June 1953
On Monday A. and I motored to stay with Elizabeth Herbert [*née* Willard, daughter of the then US Ambassador] at Tetton Park near Taunton on a strange mission. Long pre-arranged with her, it was to tackle Mr William Esdaile of Cothelstone House near Taunton. He is Shelley's great-grandson through the poet's daughter Ianthe by Harriet Westbrook. Ianthe was married by her

aunt Eliza Westbrook to Mr Esdaile of Cothelstone. The present Esdaile owns a notebook of early poems in Shelley's handwriting and/or Harriet's, and probably other undiscovered papers besides. Two years ago, staying at Tetton, I was taken to Cothelstone and shown the precious notebook by Mr Esdaile's sister who conducted me round the house, while Elizabeth walked the old boy round the garden. The sister pulled the book out of an old ottoman in the attic and I had opened it only on the first page when she snatched it from my hands and thrust it back into the ottoman because she heard her brother approaching. Mr Esdaile is an eccentric old fellow of over seventy who won't hear any reference to Shelley, either because he is ashamed of the poet for having been an atheist expelled from Oxford or because he married Harriet who came of a non-armigerous family. Neville Rogers and Edmund Blunden who are editing the complete works of Shelley for the Oxford [University] Press are very anxious to have access to the notebook in order to publish the poems, some of which have never been printed, and were missed by Edward Dowden, Shelley's first biographer. As a member of the Keats–Shelley committee I offered to help.

So on Wednesday Elizabeth took me over to Cothelstone, an astonishing house. Built about 1810 for the Esdailes as a neo-Greek villa it was added to in Victorian times. Is chock-a-block with good things and absolute trash. A landscape by Gainsborough, some portraits by Reynolds and one by Wilkie, very good, jostle among prints of puppies sheltering under umbrellas, Regency furniture and Edwardian pianolas draped with lace

tablecloths and littered with photograph frames. Nothing
has been shifted since the turn of the century. There is
somewhere a portrait of Ianthe which I saw on my
previous visit. We were ushered into Mr Esdaile's study
to wait for him. He is slight, thin-lipped, white-faced,
rather aquiline and patrician, with a stoop, not unlike
Shelley's. I dare say when young he resembled the poet
in physique. Mrs Herbert explained that we had come
early because I wished to talk to him about the notebook.
'I don't know where it is, I believe that I have lost it',
was all he said and instantly changed the subject. After
he had blamed the weather, the government, the Com-
munists, we returned to the attack. 'I believe you have
got it,' he exclaimed sharply to Elizabeth, and again
changed the subject. Finally we returned to the subject
and I asked him point-blank for permission to have it
microfilmed for the Bodleian. I quoted Blunden and
Harold Nicolson who attach immense importance to it.
'I don't like Nicolson's voice on the wireless', was the
only answer I got. But he did not positively refuse me.
Then he took us both round the garden.

At 4.30 A. and a charming American staying at Tetton,
Mrs Fenwick, joined us at a nursery tea of jam, Devonshire cream and cakes in the dining-room. They were
all wonderfully flattering and persuasive, played up to
the old man and teased him. It was time to leave so
Mrs Herbert most cunningly said she was taking the
women upstairs. I was left alone with Mr E. who I don't
suppose was a bit pleased. But I said to him, pleading, 'I
know you won't refuse my request, will you?' And he
consented to have the notebook photographed so long

as it did not leave the house. I think this was quite a successful visit.

1 July 1953

After a deal of intrigue A. and I met a photographer, sent by the Bodleian, at Taunton station this morning and drove him to Cothelstone by appointment. At last we have succeeded in photographing the Shelley notebook. It amounts to about ninety-five open pages. The poems are certainly in two handwritings, perhaps three. On the first page is inscribed the name, Ianthe Esdaile. I don't know how many poems are in Harriet's hand but I believe several are in Shelley's. I am certain a large number of the poems have never yet been printed. It was thrilling to handle once again, at leisure, the closely packed octavo volume. Mr Esdaile told me he didn't want to sell the book. I advised him to claim a reproduction fee for any poems published. He said to me: 'You must understand that until the last few years Shelley's name was never mentioned in my family. He treated my great-grandmother abominably. He even had the effrontery, while living with another woman, to ask my great-grandmother to join them in their adultery.' He said the notebook was the only relic of Shelley he possessed, apart from his christening robe. I did not ask to see this because I was so worried about getting the photographs taken. Mr E. was in a great hurry to get off for his annual holiday – the old limousine purring at the front door – and would not leave until we had finished. It was a good thing I went, for the photographer was a raw, callow youth, with no manners. Mr E. is a nice old man, old-fashioned, correct and very shy. In the dining room under the Gainsborough landscape is a hideous harmonium with *Hymns Ancient and Modern* on a music stand. Elizabeth Herbert said the squire and his sister played and sang hymns together every Sunday evening.

CUMBERLAND LODGE, *Berkshire*

A royal grace-and-favour residence in Windsor Great Park, let to Lord FitzAlan, leading Roman Catholic layman and former Viceroy of Ireland.

16–17 April 1942

I walked through Bishop's Gate into Windsor Park and was overtaken by Alathea FitzAlan-Howard on her bicycle. She is the FitzAlans' pretty daughter aged eighteen, frail and freckled. I arrived just in time for dinner for which there is no changing these days. Lord FitzAlan's son staying. It is the first time I have seen him, a tiny, rather wizened, insignificant man with a wooden leg. Magdalen [granddaughter] sad as ever, with heavy folds of tumbling, wispy hair parted in the middle of her head and looped behind anyhow. Three Grenadier officers came to dinner. They are guarding the King and Queen who are present at Royal Lodge next door. One is called Lascelles and is Blanche Lloyd's nephew, very good-looking and fair-haired, tall and 'the flower of English youth', a plant that always makes me stare and rub my eyes in admiration and envy. Both are on guard for a week, may not leave the locality, and sleep only half-undressed in the royal stables. Yet they look uncrumpled, immaculate. They seldom see the King.

Lord FitzAlan talked to me after dinner in his study about the Stanley Baldwins. S.B. is by no means a fool; is on the contrary extremely astute, and far from obstinate as is often supposed. His besetting fault is indolence. He confided in Lord F. that his reason for not rearming was that the country would not stand for it at the time.

I was given the Chapel Room, a stuffy, old-fashioned bedroom, with a huge, made-up oak bed, very comfortable with two fat rich linen pillows.

Mass in the chapel at 9. One of the Jesuits from Beaumont comes three times a week to say Mass. The Blessed Sacrament is kept in this chapel which is well arranged and furnished, unlike the usual makeshift type found in country houses. The ceremony was somehow extraordinary. There were Magdalen, Alathea, a lady's maid and one very old woman from I don't know where, all under veils. Lord FitzAlan served in spite of his eighty-seven years, shuffling about genuflecting like a two-year-old. The priest, Father Day, son of the judge in the Parnell case, is a cripple with arthritis and can barely move. He crawls at snail's pace, leaning heavily on his stick. I was in agonies lest he or Lord F. should collapse, but each supported himself on the other. Yet the scene was impressive and the recollection of it fills me with pleasure. I went to confession and as usual had to rack my brains to extract the worst sins since I last confessed, which was at Dover I believe. I find it hard to decide which are my sins. I was given 3 Paters, 3 Aves and 3 Reginas. Only Lord F. and I communicated. Lord

F. handed me a clean napkin and I trembled lest the priest, who was creaking and groaning, should drop the wafer. The wafer dissolves so foamlike in my mouth, always adhering to the roof of the mouth first of all.

I drove to Egham station with Father Day, who is an inquisitive old man, wanting to be told everything, who I am (who am I?), how I spell my name, how long I have known Cumberland Lodge and what is my age. Not an agreeable priest, and his false teeth do not fit.

DITCHLEY PARK, *Oxfordshire*

An eighteenth-century house which had been superbly decorated in the 1930s by Ronald Tree, a Conservative MP, and his American wife Nancy (whom he divorced in 1947, the lady referred to here being his second wife Marietta).

26 June 1948

Drove to Ditchley. Mrs Tree received us smilingly and charmingly. She is handsome and natural and attractive. The butler came into the big hall and asked if I would go upstairs to Ronnie Tree, in bed with a bad back. He was very friendly and asked me to come again alone, and stay. While we were talking a tall, dark figure, a trifle bent, entered quietly. He was introduced to me as Peter Beatty [son of the admiral]. I said, 'You will not remember me. We were at [Lockers Park preparatory] school together and once swapped, you a beautiful pencil and I some trashy object. I got the better of the bargain and ever since have felt guilty. We must have been nine or ten at the time.' His reply was, 'I remember it well and I remember thinking I had got the better of you. You must excuse me for not having recognized you. I am quite blind at present; only temporarily of course.' But he will, I understand, never see again.

Ditchley inside is perfection. Exquisite furniture and fabrics, many original to the house. I have never seen better taste. Nothing jars. Nothing is too sumptuous, or new. The grounds, laid out by Ronnie Tree, are suitable to the house, the outside of which is a little austere, and I regret that the two cupolas and pediment were not carried out according to Gibbs's design.

ELSING HALL, *Norfolk*

28 April 1943
Arrived at Elsing Hall late. It is a 1740s house built in square knapped flints; and has square gables typical of these parts with heraldic finials and twisted chimney-stacks. It has been unfortuntately restored in the 1850s. Nearly all the mullion windows have been replaced with plate glass. A moat completely surrounds the house. There is an open roofed hall, and an intact 1470 chapel. Mrs Thackeray and her sister Miss Clarendon Hyde are the owners, and the last of their line since the reign of Egbert. Their line was Browne, their mother being the Browne heiress. They are impoverished. They have one indoor servant only. The house is incredibly shabby, dirty and primitive. It is pathetic how within three years country people, who are unable to travel, become blind

to the squalor to which they have been reduced. In spite of the terrible *délabrement* among which they live, these ladies with their long Plantagenet pedigree, their courtesy and ease of manner, were enchanting.

FARINGDON HOUSE, *Berkshire*

Seat of the eccentric aesthete Lord Berners, who lived there with his young paramour Robert Heber-Percy, and Heber-Percy's wife and baby daughter.

26 *April* 1945

We drove [J.L.-M. and his friend Billa Harrod, wife of an Oxford don] to Faringdon. It was a day of unexcelled loveliness, the apex of springtide, warm sun and no wind. At Faringdon House Jennifer Heber-Percy was sitting in the sun, on a swing seat, against the curved retaining wall. There were small chickens running around. This frightened Billa for she hates birds. We talked until 1.45 when we lunched off chicken (she doesn't mind eating them) and rice. Lord Berners, wearing a green knitted skull cap and yellow bow tie, was positively cordial. He is a considerate host. Robert [Heber-Percy] came in to lunch from driving a tractor on the farm. He was wearing a pair of battle-dress trousers and a yellow aertex shirt open at the neck. Very bronzed by the sun, youthful and handsome. He is the *enfant terrible*, all right. What a curious family they were, sitting round this large round table. But they know how to live. I thought how enviable their *ménage*.

[Later that afternoon] found Berners alone, Billa and Jennifer having gone for a walk. He showed me round the downstairs of the house, for the Army is in occupation of the bedroom floor. Whereas the stone flags of the hall floor are worn down by generations of feet, the hard black marble ribs are not. Lord B. thinks some of the seemingly late eighteenth-century doorheads are in fact nineteenth-century and should be removed; but I am not so sure. The house is attractively untidy in an Irish way, with beds, but beautiful ones, scattered in the downstairs rooms. Much confusion and comfort combined. Jennifer's baby Victoria playing on the floor like a kitten. Lord B. said that this afternoon one of the negro soldiers – and the place is stiff with them – accosted him in the garden with the request, 'Masa, may I pick just a little bunch of flowers for our colonel?'

GREAT HAMPDEN, *Buckinghamshire*

3 July 1947
I motored to Great Hampden, arriving 11.30. Was met by Lord Buckinghamshire, aged about forty-one, whom I now remember at Eton as [Lord] Hobart. He is single, reserved, and rather charming, ugly, with a turned-up nose and moustache. He seems very much older than me, I am pleased to say. I liked him for his forthrightness and excellent manners. He offers Hampden House and about 100 acres to the Trust. The house is let to a girls' school who pay a rent of £800 a year. It is not really first rate. The property was granted to the Hampdens by

Edward the Confessor. The house dates from every period, from King John even, having two arches of his reign. The great hall with roof was brought from an old barn on the estate, the late seventeenth-century balustrade being original to the gallery. A suite of rooms in the south wing decorated *c.*1740 in Palladian style is handsome, but spoilt by use as a classroom. The staircase is Jacobean and painted with arcaded panels on the dado to give a perspective effect. The south façade is symmetrical with escutcheons in stone on the roof. The windows tame Vanbrughian. The demesne now much gone to seed. I think it is a borderline case. John Hampden of course lived and died here.

Lunched most excellently at the Hampden Arms, a tiny pub. Under the inn's name is inscribed on a board, 'The Earl of Buckinghamshire licensed to sell beer and tobacco.'

HAREWOOD HOUSE, *Yorkshire*

Seat of the 6th Earl of Harewood, who was married to the Princess Royal, sister of King George VI, and died in May 1947. Faced with massive death duties, the new Earl considered offering the house to the National Trust.

26–27 November 1947

Took the train to Leeds and arrived at one o'clock. Was met by a nice, old-fashioned chauffeur, not in livery, and a brand new small Daimler limousine with a large silver owl on the bonnet, and driven to Harewood village.

Immediately on leaving Leeds one enters the Harewood estate, on either side of the road. God, what England owes to the landed gentry for the trim appearance of their estates. Harewood village is a fine specimen of a planned eighteenth-century community. The little houses are uniform, for they were all built of a piece by John Carr. I lunched with Mr Fitzroy, the Agent. He told me the estate was faced with 75 per cent death duties, but the family were resolved to remain at Harewood notwithstanding. I suggested that the family might approach the Treasury and ask for the house, some 4,000 acres of land around it, and also the chief objects of art to be taken in lieu of death duties and handed over to the Trust. Mr F. was interested. Then he took me in his car down the Leeds road, and through the lodge gates to look at the house across the valley towards the Wharfdale and high ridge of hills beyond it. At once saw how important it was that a large area should pass with the house which is visible from such long distances.

We drove back through the main entrance, past the stable block by Chambers, to the house. Were shown into the old library to the left of the hall, and stood before a fire. While I was debating to myself how I ought to make my first obeisance, suddenly HRH [the Princess Royal] ran swiftly into the room and shook me by the hand without saying a word. When I realized who she was I just had time to incline my head. My first impression was how good looking she is, far more so than photographs suggest. She has a beautiful complexion, neat greyish hair, cropped but wavy at the back. She wore a grey tweed skirt, thick mesh wool stockings, dark leather indoor shoes, a grey jumper and one string of pearls. The effect not dowdy, but simple country dress. She is extremely shy, but dignified; sensible and natural in manner. Rather abrupt and has little small talk. When interested in a subject she becomes vivacious and communicative. It was now 3.30 and already getting dark. She took us round the state rooms until 5 o'clock. The hospital which occupied them has recently gone, and the rooms are being cleaned and put back. There were men working on the floorboards with a machine like a tennis court marker, sandpapering them. The Princess picked her way through, opening shutters, removing dust-sheets and talking affably to the workmen. In the centre library one workman was re-laying boards by the glass door, wearing his hat and smoking. When he spoke to the Princess he neither removed his hat nor his cigarette. When we left him HRH was very worried lest he set fire to the house. I thought his behaviour abominable.

Tea was in the breakfast-room, as were all meals. I always sat on the Princess's right. She kept jumping up to fill the teapot from an electric kettle. She has a smooth-haired dachshund called Bruna, to which she is devoted and with whom she keeps up a flow of banter. It sleeps in a basket in her bedroom. The other day she upset milk on the silver tray and let the dog lick it up, then, for fear of what the butler might think, washed the tray herself. Miss Lloyd and Mrs Balfour, ladies-in-waiting, were in attendance. The younger son, Gerald [Lascelles], came in from shooting. He is stocky, with large chin, slightly oafish. Has drooping, sensual mouth. He is very jolly with his mother, whom he teases.

The Princess has a remarkably beautiful deep voice, and rolls her 'r's' slightly. She has fine white teeth and a curious mark on the upper lip, as of a scald.

After tea she took FitzRoy and me to her private sitting-room where some of the best Chippendale satin-wood tables and commodes are; also a pair of Sèvres inlaid cabinets. I then explained my ideas about the Treasury scheme and she asked many questions quietly and intelligently about domestic arrangements under the National Trust. Asked if she might have a small strip of terrace to herself and dog on opening days, and proposed providing tea for the public in the stable block. 'One can get used to anything,' she observed rather pathetically. We talked until 7.40 when the Agent left us together.

My bedroom was in the semi-basement. It had a coal fire. There was no time for a bath. In fear of being late I changed quickly and dashed up to the old library just as it struck eight. At dinner there was no waiting, the Princess going first to the sideboard, helping herself, the rest following. There was plenty of banter during dinner. The P. having rung the bell for coffee said, 'Now what is the betting that they won't answer it', and two minutes later, 'I thought so.' The son then said, 'I will try, Mummie', and his peals brought a response. The P. had changed with inordinate speed into a black dress, very plain, with black shiny belt and velveteen coatee, for she is still in mourning. After dinner, sitting till nearly twelve in the old library, stifling yawns, was a bit of a trial. Talk about the crowds in buses and tubes during rush hour, the smell of human beings on a muggy, rainy day (things she can never have experienced), and then politics, and keen, anxious speculation over the Gravesend election. She says a little naively that, whatever happens, we mustn't emigrate or desert this country, however much we are tempted. I thought to myself, royalty never emigrates. It either stays put or is pushed out.

Breakfast at nine [next day]. I was up at 8.50 in case the Princess should arrive first. The ladies assembled in the breakfast-room. HRH then came in. The two ladies curtseyed and I bowed. This was all the ceremony. Every sentence has a Ma'am in it, a slightly denaturalizing suffix. And reference to her presence or absence is to Her Royal Highness. I like this. After breakfast I was allowed to walk outside on the terrace and round the house by myself. Was specially commanded to examine the small group of playing children in a painting by Baurscheit, dated 1725. I could not admire these insipidly mischievous children as much as the urns the Princess has bought at the Clumber sale and put in the Barry parterre garden. At 10.30 the Princess reappeared and until 12.20 conducted me round the house again. She takes great pride in and has considerable knowledge of the contents. Her taste, too, struck me as very good. Indeed the rooms are superb and the long gallery one of the noblest apartments I have seen in an English house. It is amazing how convincing the wooden curtain boxes are, carved to resemble drapery. The quality of the French-style Chippendale furniture the finest possible. Together we pulled off covers, compared the suites of furniture, examined ceilings, pier-glasses, door-locks and handles, chimneypieces, carpets and pictures, about which she knows a great deal. We went into every bedroom and bathroom, deploring the effects of last winter's damp on many ceilings. Went into HRH's bedroom, with large, brown, mahogany double-bed, dog's basket and dozens of photographs of Queen Mary, the late King, present monarch and family. Rather wistfully she kept saying, 'I do hope I shall not have to sell this, or that.' We even descended into the cellar to examine the china. At the end I was asked if I was tired. Valiantly I denied it, although nearly dropping, and expressed the same anxiety about her. She said she was never tired showing the house to people who appreciated it.

HINCHINGBROOKE HALL, *Huntingdon*

26 January 1946

I reached Hinchingbrooke at 1 o'clock. What a contrast to the Hollywood Anglesey Abbey. No answer from the front door bell, so I drove round to the back. Walked in and found my way through a labyrinth of passages, finally emerging into the square oak room at the corner where Hinch [Viscount Hinchingbrooke, heir to the Earl of Sandwich and MP for South Dorset] was squatting over an inadequate fire. He greeted me with, 'My dear Jimmie, has no one helped you find the way in?' He and Rosemary most welcoming. Gave me sherry and a rabbit pie cooked by Rosemary, for the staff consists of army batmen and wives, and no cook. The Hinchingbrookes are picnicking in the house, still full of hospital beds and furniture. The hospital has only just vacated. Hinch took me round the outside and inside of the house. The gatehouse and nunnery, with gables, and the large 1692 bay window are the best features. Hinch has contracted for £400 to have the 1880 wing of red brick pulled down, also the ugly pepper-box tower of that date. This will make the house far more manageable and improve its appearance. It will also reveal the nunnery from the gardens, all sloping gently down to a lake with fine elm trees close to the house. The raised terrace overlooking the road is a Jacobean conceit. There is absolutely nothing to see inside the house, apart from the Charles II dado of the staircase.

At 3.30 I found Rosemary on her knees scrubbing the kitchen floor, and I helped her to swab it over. The kind Hinchingbrookes made me stay the night in the house, so I cancelled my room at the inn. Very cold and most primitive bathroom with no mat, no soap, etc. Rosemary a true bohemian, untidy and slapdash, and for this reason admirable, and tough. She is like a very jolly able-bodied seaman. Has four children and intends to have lots more. After dinner she showed me the contents of the crops of pigeons shot that afternoon. Gave a precise anatomical lecture as she tore open their guts, squeezing out undigested acorns and berries. Then started on the gizzards and stomachs, by which time I felt rather sick and turned away. She has studied medicine and wanted to become a qualified doctor, but Hinch put a stop to that.

HOLKHAM HALL, *Norfolk*

19 June 1947

I would definitely put Holkham among the first twenty great houses of England. With its collections it forms one very great work of art indeed. Lord Leicester is a charming and cultivated man. There were, besides Michael [Lord Rosse, friend of J.L.-M. and member of Country House Committee] and me, [Lady] Sylvia [Combe, Lord L.'s daughter, married to J.L.-M.'s former wartime commanding officer], Lord L. and his son, Tommy [Viscount] Coke, a nice, weak person, and my contemporary. Delicious dinner of cold venison eaten in a low-ceilinged, long room on the ground floor between the family and the strangers' wings. I sat next to Lord Leicester who said how disappointed he was that the family entail prevented him handing over Holkham. His last words to me were: 'If you can find any means whereby the Trust can take over this house and its contents, I shall be prepared to leave it, should my not staying on make the transfer easier.' After dinner we walked round the house. The high quality of the architecture and contents takes the breath away. The planning too is astonishingly convenient. There are four complete wings detached from the centre block. Yet when inside the house you get the impression that there are no breaks and the five entities makes one house, huge though it be. You get vistas from one wing through the centre block into another wing, conveying a surprising effect of grandeur. The other impression made upon me was the marmoreal, classical simplicity of unadorned wall spaces contrasting with the rich ornamentation of ceilings and doorways and fireplaces. The sculpture gallery in particular struck me in this way – so pure, correct and serene. We spent some little time at the end of the tour in the library where I was chiefly interested in the detailed account book kept by the first Lord Leicester who amassed his collections before the age of twenty-five. Lady Leicester is away, staying in Sylvia's house, with a nervous breakdown brought on by the anxiety and worry of keeping up Holkham with practically no servants. What these wretched landowners have to go through! Yet Holkham is superbly kept up, all the steel grates, for instance, shining brightly, the work of one devoted daily.

HOLLAND HOUSE, *Kensington*

The owner, Lord Ilchester, was in the process of donating this historic London house with its famous park to the National Trust when it was bombed in the Blitz.

5 February 1942
A horrid day in London. Cold intense, and a bitter wind blowing nasty wet snow in one's face. The SPAB [Society for the Protection of Ancient Buildings] office in Great Ormond Street is almost the only building left standing in this devastated area. All round, where whole squares and streets of houses existed a short time ago, are now empty blankets of snow. The meeting had already begun, with Lord Esher in the chair. The chief item on the

agenda was Holland House. It appears that the whole interior is gutted, and the staircase is rotting in the rain and snow. Everything else has gone except the walls, which in my opinion are no longer Jacobean, for the windows, copings, etc. were largely Victorianized. I submitted that the chief point about Holland House was its historical associations, which have now gone for ever. Anyway, the Ilchesters will never live in it again, and I feel sure that the £37,000 needed to rebuild it will not be forthcoming after the war. The prospect of a twentieth-century Jacobean fake is surely worse than a Victorian Jacobean fake.

28 April 1942
At 11 Ted Lister [country-house-owning friend of J.L.-M.] called for me and I took him to Holland House. We walked in at the gates and right up to the house where we talked to the caretaker, who had been on the spot when the house had burnt about a year ago. It is a shell. The only part remaining, though badly damaged, is oddly enough the Jacobean staircase, with one of the Jacobean doorways leading to it. The Spanish leather under the stairs still hanging in festoons from the walls. A sedan chair and a small lacquer chest, half-burnt, are left. The painted panelled room for Charles I which I remember Lord Ilchester once showing me is gone. We could just distinguish where it had been, for I saw traces of one painted pilaster. The library and everything else irretrievably gone. I am glad I once visited this house, and danced in it, in its heyday. Ted and I walked along the terraces, through the old walled garden and

northwards through the park, and down a long lime avenue. The grass was long and unmown, but the trees were fresh and re-budding, quite indifferent to the terrible indignities of last year. The tranquillity made it difficult for us to realize we were in the centre of London. How important it is to preserve what remains of this sanctuary.

INVERARAY CASTLE, *Argyll*

Seat of the Duke of Argyll. J.L.-M.'s friend Geoffrey Houghton Brown, who knew the Duke, took Jim for a holiday there in 1943.

18 September 1943
We caught the 8.45 bus [from Glasgow] to Inveraray. Loch Lomond was glassy calm and the water blue-grey like my lady's eyes of yesterday. This is my great-grandmother McFarlane's country and the beginning of the Highlands. When we reached the Pass the sun came out fitfully and spread a gold and purple patchwork on the hills. At Loch Fyne sun and sky and water were Mediterranean. As the bus turned a corner I had my first view of Inveraray, a wide bay in the loch with little boats and large ships in the harbour, and a minute classical town in the background. Then I saw the gaunt, grey block of the castle, the two classical bridges and the romantic peaked hill with watch tower upon it. A man from the castle met us on the quay and wheeled our luggage on a trolley. We followed him through a gate

and to avoid the soldiery whose huts are in the park, along the drive and among the shrubs, we took a path through the desolate garden, and crossed a bridge over the moat straight into the great saloon.

The castle is built of ugly stone, which turns grey in the sunlight and black in the rain. This is a pity, for all the old houses in the town are of a lighter, kindlier stone. The castle has been greatly spoilt by peaked dormer windows added in 1880, and unsightly chimneys stuck on turrets and steeples. Outside it is grim and forbidding like some hydropathic hotel. The bridge to the front door had a sloping shelter erected over it for the benefit of Queen Victoria. Geoffrey led me through the saloon to the library where the Duke of Argyll was writing. He was seated at a large table in the middle of the room, with a bronze replica of a Celtic cross and one lighted candle on it. He rose and was very welcoming. He is obviously fond of Geoffrey.

He is a short old man with white hair and a smooth white face, for he seldom if ever has to shave. He has handsome blue eyes. He has a woman's voice, very eunuchy. He was wearing an old Harris tweed, deer-red jacket, with wide button revers up the sleeves, and immensely old tartan kilt, old blue woollen stockings (revealing white knobbly knees), dirk, sporran, and most surprising of all, shoes *à l'espadrille*. He conducted us up a long, stone staircase with plain iron baluster curves for crinolines, and threadbare carpet. The central hall, exceedingly high, reaches to the roof of the central tower. High though it is, it always retains a smell of lodging-house cooking. Windows are never opened, and no wonder, for the castle is bitterly cold in September without fires. My small bedroom is just over the front door. It has double doors, with a moth-eaten, red rep curtain over the inner one. On the blue-and-white wallpaper hang a large framed photograph of the widowed Queen Victoria (looking like Robert Byron) at the time of the first Jubilee, a large oil of an eighteenth-century duke in a beautiful rococo frame, and a foxed print of the Porteous Riots. The Victorian iron bedstead has a red plush covered canopy. The washstand, dressing-table and clothes cupboard are solid Victorian mahogany pieces. A fire is actually burning in the grate – rather feebly. There is a lovely view from my window (which has not been cleaned for years) of the watch tower hill and a corner of the loch.

We had a delicious luncheon of mackerel and grouse, helping ourselves from the sideboard. The duke is very voluble and he has an insatiable appetite for gossip, as well as food. Conversation revolves round people and their relationships. After luncheon he put on a Glengarry green with age, and set off to the hospital in the park with some French newspapers for wounded French Canadian troops. A soldier on guard stopped us going up the long ride. 'What's this? I can go where I like. I am the duke', came from a high-pitched, slightly hysterical voice. From the hospital Geoffrey and I went on to the little eighteenth-century fishing lodge by the first fall, looking for salmon. I saw one leaping, but the wrong way, not upstream but down. We continued up the burn, the Aray I presume, crossed over a bridge where I pointed to a rock in midstream like a surrealist sculpture of a torso with one buttock incomplete, and bitten away. We tested each other on the trees we passed. I failed over a sycamore and a rowan. We found the eighteenth-century pigeon house which is at the end of the vista.

Meals here are excellent in that solid Scotch way I love – porridge, bannocks, plum cakes and game. The duke prattles as ceaselessly as the Aray flows over the stones. Sometimes he is very entertaining; sometimes he is boring, and one does not listen. It makes no difference to him. He is a recognized authority on all church ritual, and a scholar of medieval liturgy, hagiology and Saxon coins. He is eccentric. He will rush without warning out of the room to play a bar or two of a Gregorian chant on a harmonium, or to play on a gong, or a French horn. He also has a cuckoo whistle which he likes to blow in the woods in order to bewilder the soldiers. He takes the keenest interest in the soldiers, both officers and men, learns their names and where they come from, and the names of their diocese and bishop. The great advantage of this place is that after meals the duke disappears, and we are left to read, write, walk out of doors, or roam round the house.

After tea we looked at the rooms on the ground floor. Great bushes of laurel and ungainly spruce trees have been allowed to grow close to the house, with the result that the magnificent views from all sides are shut out. Geoffrey once suggested their being felled, but the duke would not hear of it. It is true that today they serve as screens against the myriad Nissen huts. In the lower part of the hall are two ugly fireplaces. Over them and indeed all the way up the walls practically to the roof are ranged archaic weapons, guns, rifles, pistols, spears and daggers, in giant Catherine wheel patterns. Elks' horns are interspersed. In the blank spaces are numerous family portraits. On one chimneypiece stands a bronze equestrian effigy of Richard Coeur de Lion by Princess Louise [Queen Victoria's daughter, who had married the Duke's uncle and predecessor], 'my aunt'. The state rooms on this floor contain some splendid eighteenth-century furniture and on the rose damask walls of the saloon portraits by Gainsborough, Cotes and Batoni hung higgledy-piggledy. Amongst other things is the most astonishing bric-à-brac, including a forest of framed photographs collected by 'my aunt'.

KELMSCOTT MANOR, *Gloucestershire*

Home of the artist, writer and political radical William Morris (1834–96).

11 *July* 1942

After tea, we bicycled over the fields and across the river to Kelmscott. The old, grey stone gables are first seen through the trees. The house is surrounded by a dovecote and farm buildings which are still used by a farmer. The romantic group must look exactly as it did when William Morris found it lying in the low water meadows, quiet and dreaming. It is like an etching by F. L. Griggs. The garden is divine, crammed with flowers wild and tangled, an enchanted orchard garden for there are fruit trees and a mulberry planted by Morris. All the flowers are as Pre-Raphaelite as the house, being rosemary, orange-smelling lilies, lemon-scented verbena. The windows outside have small pediments over them. Inside there are Charles II chimneypieces, countryfied by rude Renaissance scrolls at the base of the jambs. The interior is redolent of Morris and Rossetti, yet not the least nineteenth century, which speaks loudly for their taste. Most of the rooms have Morris wallpapers, and contain many framed drawings by them both, of Mrs Morris and the children. The room in which Morris worked has a great four-poster. Rossetti's room is lined with the tapestries which, when the wind blew them about, worried him and induced nightmares. I like bad old tapestries to be chopped about and treated as wallpaper. They make a superb background to the pictures. I leant out of the casement window, unlike the Lady of Shalott, and gazed across the flat, meadowy landscape and the winding river which looked so comfortable and serene. I do not remember experiencing such sweet peace and happiness as during these two hours.

KNEBWORTH MANOR, *Hertfordshire*

Owned by the grandson of the Victorian novelist-statesman Bulwer Lytton, who had built it.

13 June 1942
I took a bus to Knebworth where I was met by the agent and motored to Knebworth Manor. Lord Lytton pompous, courteous in a keep-your-distance manner,

patrician and vice-regal. He was wearing rather precious country clothes, a too immaculate tweed suit, a yellow-green shirt of large checks loose at the collar, and a gold chain round his neck. He has truly beautiful blue eyes. If one did not know otherwise one would suppose him to be what my father calls 'effeminate' by the well-cut yet long silver hair deliberately curled round the nape of his neck.

We walked through the gardens of Knebworth House. It is undeniably hideous. The old house was rebuilt by Bulwer Lytton in 1847, and if only Lord Lytton had not recently removed the gargoyles from the absurd turrets and the heraldic animals from the terrace, it would be a perfect specimen of a Disraelian Gothic mansion. The whole outside is stuccoed in a base way. The Jacobean grand staircase and the Presence Chamber are terribly shoddy. The only room I liked was the Palladianized great hall. Lord Lytton has had the paint stripped off the wainscote. He said it was the first stripping to be undertaken in England. At present the Froebel Girls' College is installed in the house, which becomes them. Lord Lytton is determined to return to the house after the war. I insisted on going round the estate for he offers the whole 3,000 acres in endowment. My view is that the estate is more worth holding, because of its near-ness to London, than the house, for all its historic associations.

MADRESFIELD COURT, *Worcestershire*

The house which inspired Eveyln Waugh to write Brideshead
Revisited – *in which the character of 'Bridey' is obviously
inspired by the Lord Beauchamp described here.*

20 July 1948

Lunched at Madresfield. Lord Beauchamp is fat, with a
great paunch, looking like God knows what, wearing
an old blue shirt, open at the frayed neck, and a tight
pair of brown Army shorts, baby socks and sandshoes.
Lady B. plump, but pretty. The house is not in my eyes
beautiful. The situation, however, is made beautiful by
the Malvern Hills looming over it. You approach it by a
straight drive of more than a mile, but the actual estate
is on flat and dull ground. The gardens (there are ten
gardeners) are delicious, especially the long avenues and
paths, and the arboretum, busts of Roman emperors
under arches of yew close to the house, which is moated.
The contents are marvellous – pictures and sixteenth-
century portraits. As for the miniatures, of which there
are a great number, they are superlative. Also some
good French furniture and many bibelots; snuff boxes,
gold, silver, bejewelled, etc. One could spend hours
here enjoying these things which by themselves make
Madresfield worthy of preservation for all time.

We lunched in the great hall – much altered eighty
years ago. It faces a little central court, half-timbered in
a Nürnberg manner. Lady Beauchamp is a Dane and her
two stepdaughters and old mother, who does not speak

and to whom one does not speak, were staying. Lord and
Lady B. spent all afternoon conducting and explaining. A
picnic tea was had by the swimming pool. Then he took
me to see two half-timbered lesser houses on the estate.
The rich tenants from the Black Country most obsequi-
ous, and apologetic to the Earl for not being in their best
clothes, whereas he was dressed as described. Earls with
sores on their knees should not parade them exposed to
their villeins. In spite of his fatness and unshaven porky
face, his manner is patrician and stiff.

MELTON CONSTABLE HALL, *Norfolk*

15 May 1942

At Melton Constable we were welcomed most kindly by
Lord Hastings, who is living in the stable wing, lateral
to the main block. He is a sort of Edwardian stage peer
with a purple visage. He is vastly proud of the place and
has recently celebrated his family's 700th anniversary
of their lordship of Melton Constable, unbroken from
father to son, which is remarkable. He prefaced his
reception of us with a resumé of his family honours and
connections. His ignorance of the house's architecture
was however startling. He kept dogmatizing pompously,
and wrongly, about this and that feature. The house is
ruined to my mind by the 1880s additions. They could
easily be pulled down so as to leave the lovely 'Wren'
block intact. But Lord Hastings prefers them to the
original house. A pity that it has lost its roof balustrade
and cupola. We looked at the church in the park. It

contains a Caroline family pew hugely out of proportion to the nave, and an ugly war memorial to the men of Melton Constable, headed by the name in large letters of The Hon. — Astley, followed underneath by the names in smaller letters of the humble privates and gunners of the village.

NETHER LYPIATT MANOR, *Gloucestershire*

30 March 1944
Started off in the NT car at 10 o'clock for Gloucestershire and drove without a break to Nether Lypiatt Manor, near Stroud, to lunch at this wonderful little house with Mrs Gordon Woodhouse [the eminent harpsichordist]. There were Mr Woodhouse, a little, dull old man with a flabby hand, genial Lord Barrington with hairs growing out of his cheeks and ears, and homespun Miss Walker, daughter of Sir Emery, the friend of William Morris. The house is perched high on a hill, overlooking a built-up village. It is compact and tall, with two flanking wings, one new so as to balance the other old one. It is unspoilt late seventeenth century, and perfect in every way. In fact an ideal, if not *the* ideal small country house. It retains all its wainscoting, doors with high brass handles and locks, one lovely chimneypiece in the hall, of white stone against a ground of blue slate. The rich staircase has three twisted balusters to each tread. There is much good furniture, and several Barrington family portraits. The forecourt enclosure with stone piers and balls, the

contemporary wrought-iron gates, and the Cotswold stable block complete the dependencies.

Mrs Woodhouse was wearing a kind of black satin bonnet, not becoming, and a black knitted dress. Luncheon consisted of one egg in a jacketed potato. The boiler having just burst the household was in a state of perturbation. There is one servant. It is a curious colony. After luncheon, Mrs Woodhouse and Lord Barrington took me round the house, and he took me round the garden, which is enchanting, with modern yew walks and a flourishing young lime avenue, the trees planted closely together. There is an obelisk to the horse of the builder of the house who 'served his master good and true, and died at the age of forty-two'.

OCKWELLS MANOR, *Berkshire*

22 February 1942
From High Wycombe I bussed to Bray Wick and from there walked to Ockwells Manor. I was last here in 1936. My host, Sir Edward Barry, now eighty-four, is as lively as ever. He has one servant. Sir Edward himself stokes the boiler every morning. The house is sadly dusty. We had a delicious English roast beef luncheon with Yorkshire pudding, rhubarb tart to follow. A gin and vermouth warmed me first of all, for it is still bitterly cold. Sir Edward wants to sell. He owns 600 acres with a rental of £1,200 and is asking £75,000 because an American millionaire offered him that figure ten or more years

ago. He spurned Cook's [the philanthropist Ernest Cook who bought worthwhile properties and donated them to the NT] offer of £40,000. I fear I cannot help him unless he changes his tune. He took me round the house again. Although it is most important, yet it does not please. Sir E. is 2nd baronet and Baron du Barry in Portugal, which is strange.

5 April 1973

Yesterday I visited Ockwells in Berkshire. The first time I went there was in 1936, the then owner being Sir Edward Barry. The result was covenants over the house and estate, but no gift to the National Trust. Sir Edward wanted to give, but could not afford to do so. He had two married daughters, as I remember, neither of whom was very rich. In those days Ockwells was generally considered a very important house indeed. It was written up in all the architectural textbooks, as a mid-fifteenth-century manor house of the earliest non-fortified sort, of much importance. Sir Edward extensively restored it before the First World War with the help and advice of people like Lutyens, Edward Hudson [owner of *Country Life*] and Avary Tipping [architectural journalist]. No one disputed its merits. Yesterday, however, John Cornforth [architectural historian] and Christopher Wall [NT official], who accompanied me, expressed the view that Ockwells was an over-restored fake, beastly in every way, and not worthy to be held by the National Trust. Thus I have lived to see taste change. Ockwells was never the sort of house I cared for, yet in the 1930s I did not dream of questioning its importance.

OMBERSLEY COURT, *Worcestershire*

22 October 1948

This morning Papa and I motored to Ombersley, the first time I have ever been inside the house. We were asked to go there by Lord Sandys, who has just succeeded his cousin, dead at the age of ninety. The present lord is seventy-two and as Colonel Hill was a friend of my father. He and his wife charming and hospitable. In return for asking me to wander round the house and assess the contents (a curious request) he gave me a present of four pots of honey, some pears and a box of cigars. The front of the house facing the road is dull Grecian *c.*1810, with plain portico, added in stone by the Marchioness of Downshire, the last Sandys in her own right, to a William and Mary house behind. The old house consists of a central hall comprising two storeys, a gallery connecting the upstairs bedrooms, and a ponderous ceiling of the 1810 period. The bedrooms all wainscoted in oak of William and Mary time with nice panelled doors and brass locks and handles. Handsome staircase of three balusters to each tread. One corner room contains elaborately raised door-cases with small pediments. It is a treasure house, full of good, but not exceptional, and some junky, things. Many portraits of Sandyses, one mid-sixteenth-century portrait of Sir John Cheek, a good Jansens of George Sandys, poet and traveller, a charming Dobson of a Sandys and Prince Rupert at a junketing, Sandys dipping the ribbon of a third disaffected friend's hat in the Prince's glass of claret. A delightful portrait of

Lady Downshire [ancestress], her little foot peeping out of her skirts and resting on a footstool. There is some nice Regency furniture in the bedrooms, the remains of a George II state bed, of splendid red Genoa velvet, but mutilated. Several gilt gesso mirrors and gilt gesso tables of Queen Anne date, very good indeed.

We were given a picnic luncheon with sherry and white wine. Lord and Lady S. have not moved in yet.

PITCHFORD HALL, *Shropshire*

A splendid black-and-white manor house.

17 March 1944

Hired a car for £1 to take me to Pitchford Hall. A most glorious day, though keen and sharp. The black-and-white of this house is a bit too much of a good thing. The house is supposed to be late fifteenth or early sixteenth century, but I suspect it to be much later. The clock-tower porch is obviously Jacobean. The north wing extension of 1880 is well done, but over-contributes to the black-and-white. However, today the place looked highly romantic amid the buds of spring, flowering crocuses and primroses. Met Forsyth, the architect, in the drive who told me Sir Charles Grant was waiting for me. Was conducted upstairs to a small, shapeless end room in the west wing, where he sprawled, listening to the European news in the way country people do most of the livelong day. He is well over 60, still handsome, and rather mischievous. Indeed a sweet man who must once have been attractive. He is an old friend of that fellow general, Lord Sackville. Eddy tells me that he remembers that, at Knole, years ago, the two men were discussing something rather excitedly. Lord Sackville said, 'What you can't understand, Charlie darl . . .', and stopped dead. Too late, Eddy [Sackville-West]'s mother, who was present, rose from her chair and stalked out of the room, head in air.

Now Sir Charles vegetates, and talks volubly and a little irrelevantly about his ancestors, his friends and acquaintances. He galloped me through the house, pointing out the contents which he thought he would give with it. But so rapid was our progress that I could not take in individual things. I don't think there is much that is very good. The rooms have a rather incongruous early Victorian air, which is sad and romantic. All the rooms are low and dark in spite of the sun shining outside, the birds singing and the water falling over the stones. He dearly loves the place. His proposals are vague, however, and he does not intend to transfer any land over and above what the house stands on, even omitting the orangery and walled garden.

While he was talking to me on the lawn Lady Sibyl [Grant, daughter of the Prime Minister Lord Rosebery] approached. Out of the corner of my eye I saw a fat, dumpy figure waddling and supporting herself with a tall stick. She wore a long blue coat down to her calves. One foot had on a stocking, the other was bare. On her head was an orange bonnet, draped with an orange scarf which floated down to her ankles. She had orange hair kept in place by a wide-meshed blue net. She took care to shield her extraordinary face, extraordinary because, although she is beautiful, the shape is absolutely round and the lips are the vividest orange I have ever beheld. She looks like a clairvoyante preserved in ectoplasm. As a special favour she took me to the orangery where she lives, for she hates the house, which she says is haunted. She cannot sleep on the east side for the noise of the water, or on the north because of the graveyard. She and Sir Charles send messages to each other throughout the day and night, and meet for coffee on the lawn when weather permits. She would not allow Forsyth to come near the orangery, which is her sanctum, converted by her into one large living-room with a wood fire, and one bedroom. She talked incessantly for an hour, complaining how the aeroplanes swooped so low that she lost her voice and was obliged to move into a caravan in a ploughed field to escape them. Said that her French maid 'never revealed she was mad' when she came to her, and stole all her clothes. The only way she recovered them was to send the maid to confession – the abbess made her give them all back. Her gruff laugh and low, sepulchral voice reminded me of Lady Crewe, her sister. She had sprained her ankle – hence the one bare leg – and made me pour a solution of Ponds Extract over it out of a heavy lead Marie Antoinette watering can.

PYRLAND HALL, *Somerset*

3 February 1943

I had a horrible day with Colonel Pemberton at Pyrland Hall near Taunton. He is a fiendish old imbecile with a grotesque white moustache. When I first saw him he was pirouetting on his toes in the road. He has an inordinate opinion of himself and his own judgement. He is absolutely convinced that Pyrland is the finest house in Somerset and he is doing the Trust a great service in bequeathing it. The truth is the property does not comprise land of outstanding natural beauty and is of insignificant size; moreover the house, though large, and basically eighteenth century, has been thoroughly Victorianized as to windows and rendering. The army occupies it at present. It has a nice Georgian staircase and some plaster cornices and mahogany doors on the curve. I was drawn into several acrimonious arguments with the old man, whom I cordially disliked, for he insisted upon contradicting whatever I said. He gave me an exiguous lunch of bread and cheese, both hard as wood, a baked potato in its skin, dry as sawdust, and watery apple pie with Bird's custard. Ugh! He expected me to return and waste the following day in discussion. But I had already made up my mind after the first half-hour of my visit. I could not have borne him or Pyrland an hour longer. Having hated me like poison he was nevertheless furious when I left at 4. I conclude that he has to have some victim on whom he can vent his spleen.

RAGLEY HALL, *Warwickshire*

19 October 1948

On leaving Alcester I drove to Ragley up the Worcester drive, not the Arrow drive. Arrived 3 o'clock. The house stands on an eminence and the ground slopes from all four sides. This is unusual. Consequently there are distant views from each front. Moreover there are no modern annexes to mar the house, which was built in 1683 by a Seymour. My hostess told me the architect is thought to be Robert Hooke. I should have guessed Talman or Francis Smith for it has affinities with Dyrham or Sutton Scarsdale. The material is blue lias stone, of the off-Cotswold, Bidford-on-Avon variety, and some sandstone, which has perished, notably the dentils of the cornice. The great columned portico may be of later date than the house. You enter by an opening below the perron (added by Wyatt) and, as at Kedleston, pass into an undercroft.

Lady Helen Seymour was awaiting me in the library. She is tall, about fifty-eight, with lovely blue eyes, and must have been a beauty. *Très grande dame*. Was the youngest daughter of the 1st Duke of Westminster. Her son, Lord Hertford, the owner of Ragley, is only eighteen, and has just left Eton. She showed me over house and grounds. The great hall magnificent, now quite empty. The stucco-work might be by Gibbs's Italians, or even the Italian who worked at Ragley, called Vassali. The other rooms on this floor have rococo ceilings of 1740 or thereabouts, which Lady H. believes to be original, and later ceilings in a thin Adamish style with small round grisaille cameos, perhaps by Holland, but this is all guesswork. I have as yet read nothing about the house. In the library is a large Reynolds of Horace Walpole as a young man. He was a cousin of Marshal Conway, a Seymour, to whom he was devoted. There is a Reynolds of him too. Altogether some eight Reynoldses. There are magnificent Chippendale hall benches, the finest I have seen; two panels of carved fruit in the library which might be by Gibbons; some Louis XV marquetry commodes; a huge bed under a dust-sheet or, rather, very pretty chintz curtain, so that I could not see it, in the Royal Bedroom that once had lacquer wallpaper. The woodwork is still painted black and gold. Doorcases and dados are nearly all 1683. There are excellent Morlands and a huge Wootton of three packs of hounds meeting at Ragley. I think it is one of the most interesting great houses I have seen. The stables are enchanting, built round two courtyards. The laundry yard has a colonnade. The lower courtyard is elliptical. Lady Helen fears they will have to leave the house and move to a smaller one on the estate. Heating is a great problem and they have only two servants, one Swiss. I liked her much.

STRATFIELD SAYE, *Hampshire*

Bought by a grateful nation for the great Duke of Wellington after Waterloo. J.L.-M.'s friend Lord 'Gerry' Wellesley, an architect involved in the conservation work of the National

Trust, succeeded as the 7th Duke following the death in action of his nephew in 1943.

15 April 1944

I caught the 1.15 to Reading where Gerry Wellington met me at the station in his small car, for he gets twenty gallons a month for being a duke. Arriving at the entrance to Stratfield Saye park we stopped at the first duke's great polished granite pillar, with his image by Marochetti standing on the top. It is carefully executed, and the huge blocks of granite are finely cut. Stopped again at the 1750 church, of Greek cruciform. A Wellington monument by Flaxman, and another by Boehm. The great galleried family pew in which the Iron Duke worshipped was swept away by an ignorant vicar just before Gerry succeeded, greatly to his annoyance, for he had been looking forward to worshipping in it.

The western view of Stratfield Saye house clearly shows it to date from Charles I's reign. The original red brick was covered with a dull compo rendering in the eighteenth century, which is a pity. Odd pilasters resting on nothing appear upon the first storey in typical Charles I non-style. The house is low-lying, unpretentious, having been built, as an early guide book puts it, 'for convenience rather than for parade', by the Rivers family. They made alterations in the 1740s and added a wing in the 1790s. Benjamin Wyatt carried out work for the first duke, and added the porch and conservatory. The east front is not so regular as the west, and the terraces are deformed by messy Edwardian flower beds. Gerry, who hates flowers, will soon have them away. The pleasure grounds contain fine specimens of every tree, hard wood and soft. Under a tree is Copenhagen's gravestone. The heavy gilded state coach in the coach-house is in splendid condition.

Having eaten little luncheon I was famished, but tea consisted of only a few of the thinnest slices of bread and butter imaginable. After tea we did a tour of the inside of the house, beginning with the hall. When my stomach started to rumble with hunger Gerry looked at it with a reproachful air, and said nothing. It went on making the most awful noise like a horse's. The hall has a gallery along the wall opposite the entrance. The open balusters were boxed in so as to prevent the servants being seen from below by the visitors. Gerry's mother used to say that nothing of them was visible except their behinds, as they crouched and bobbed across the gallery. There are some pictures so huge that they can only hang sloping. In the flagged floor are inset two large mosaic pavements from Silchester. The whole hall is painted nineteenth-century brown and the walls are hung with very faded red flock paper. Against the columns of the gallery are plinths supporting white marble busts of Pitt, the Russian Czars, Walter Scott and the Great Duke.

The Gallery is long and low – 'matey' Gerry calls it – the walls covered with prints pasted upon a ground of gold leaf. Rather attractive, but G. wishes to cover these walls with damask, without however injuring the prints but so as to allow room for family portraits, for else-where there is singularly little space. At either end of the Gallery are brown painted columns, forming screens. The ceilings are covered with Edwardian lodging-house lincrusta. To the north is a small room with niches. The walls are hung with a delightful, flowery, 1850 gold and cream paper. In front of the fireplace is a special device of the Great Duke, namely a curious brass rail, with rings for curtains, to keep off excessive heat. The drawing-room has a rococo ceiling, and some Boule cabinets and commodes by Levasseur and pictures acquired by the first duke. The dining-room is shut up, all the Apsley House pictures being stored there for the war, and valued at a million pounds, so G. says. The library is of Lord Burlington date. In it are the Duke's library chairs as seen in the conversation piece by Thorburn of this room, hanging in the Small Cabinet Room. Beyond it a billiard table and Regency lights for colza oil, very pretty, and beyond again the Great Duke's private rooms and his original bath. These rooms G. is going to make his own. The bath is very deep and satisfactory. A curious feature of this house is the water closets in each room, put there by the Great Duke inside great 1840-ish cupboards of maplewood.

After tea Gerry took a rod, and fished in the lake for perch with a minnow, but caught nothing. He cast with much ease and abandon. When I tried, I made rather a fool of myself. After dinner, at which there were no drinks except beer, he showed me his grandfather's collection of gems and intaglios, mounted on long, gold chains. When held against the oil lights, some of the stones were very beautiful. G. is very fussy over the key bunches, everything being carefully locked up. He has a butler, cook and two housemaids, and a secretary, Miss Jones. The last has meals with him during the week, and nearly drives him mad with her archness. 'Aren't you naughty today?' she says. She is unable to type, so when he wishes to despatch a letter not written by himself, he types it and gives it to her to sign.

TREDEGAR HOUSE, *Monmouth*

9 November 1949

I left early this morning for Newport, Monmouthshire. Was met at the station by John Morgan [heir to 5th Baron Tredegar], flying his personal flag on the radiator of his motor, and driven to Tredegar. He is absurdly pompous and puffed up with self-importance, yet has a genuine sense of duty, and his religion means everything to him. We spent the afternoon going round the house. Now it *is* important, and probably the best in Wales. Nevertheless I was a trifle disappointed by the coarse, unrefined quality of the craftsmanship. Some of the contents are superb, notably the French furniture and in particular the Adam bureau-cum-harpsichord all in one, with a clock in the pediment. John showed me the figures of his estimated income after he has paid death duties, which amount to 80 per cent. His gross income is £40,000. After paying tax it will be reduced to £3,700, and he cannot spend his capital because it is all in trust. I slept in the panelled room in the bed said to be Mary Queen of Scots', but I wonder. John is very dogmatic about his possessions and at the same time ignorant, like many owners. He told me that on clearing his cousin Evan's bedroom cupboard he came upon 'instruments of the most bloodcurdling nature'. He took them gingerly between finger and thumb and threw them in the dust-bin. I said that in doing this he gave the dustmen ample opportunity of circulating scandalous gossip about the family. John forebore to tell me what the 'instruments' were.

WENTWORTH WOODHOUSE, *Yorkshire*

As an act of sheer class-war vindictiveness, the Labour government decided in 1946 to destroy the park of this magnificent house, seat of the Earls Fitzwilliam, by carrying out open-cast coal-mining there.

26 May 1946

Left at ten from King's Cross to Doncaster. Michael [Earl of] Rosse [of the Country Houses Committee] met me and motored me to Wentworth Woodhouse. Had time to walk round the outside and over parts of the inside. It is certainly the most enormous private house I have ever beheld. I could not find my way about the interior and never once knew in what direction I was looking from a window. Strange to think that until 1939 one man lived in the whole of it. All the contents are put away or stacked in heaps in a few rooms, the pictures taken out of their frames. The dirt is appalling. Everything is pitch black and the boles of the trees like thunder. To my surprise the park is not being worked for coal systemati-cally, but in square patches here and there. One of these patches is a walled garden. Right up to the very wall of the Vanbrugh front every tree and shrub has been uprooted, awaiting the onslaught of the bulldozers. Where the surface has been worked is waste chaos and, as Michael said, far worse than anything he saw of French battlefields after D-day. I was surprised too by the very high quality of the pre-Adam rooms and ceilings of Wentworth; by the amount of seventeenth-century work surviving; by the beautiful old wallpapers; and by the vast scale of the lay-out of the park, with ornamental temples sometimes one-and-a-half miles or more away. Lady Fitzwilliam in a pair of slacks, rather dumpy and awkward, came downstairs for a word just before we left. I fancy she is not very sensitive to the tragedy of it all.

THE STORY OF PENGUIN CLASSICS

Before 1946 ...'Classics' are mainly the domain of academics and students, without readable editions for everyone else. This all changes when a little-known classicist, E. V. Rieu, presents Penguin founder Allen Lane with the translation of Homer's Odyssey that he has been working on and reading to his wife Nelly in his spare time.

1946 The Odyssey becomes the first Penguin Classic published, and promptly sells three million copies. Suddenly, classic books are no longer for the privileged few.

1950s Rieu, now series editor, turns to professional writers for the best modern, readable translations, including Dorothy L. Sayers's *Inferno* and Robert Graves's *The Twelve Caesars*, which revives the salacious original.

1960s 1961 sees the arrival of the Penguin Modern Classics, showcasing the best twentieth-century writers from around the world. Rieu retires in 1964, hailing the Penguin Classics list as 'the greatest educative force of the 20th century'.

1970s A new generation of translators arrives to swell the Penguin Classics ranks, and the list grows to encompass more philosophy, religion, science, history and politics.

1980s The Penguin American Library joins the Classics stable, with titles such as *The Last of the Mohicans* safeguarded. Penguin Classics now offers the most comprehensive library of world literature available.

1990s Penguin Popular Classics are launched, offering readers budget editions of the greatest works of literature. Penguin Audiobooks brings the classics to a listening audience for the first time, and in 1999 the launch of the Penguin Classics website takes them online to an ever larger global readership.

The 21st Century Penguin Classics are rejacketed for the first time in nearly twenty years. This world famous series now consists of more than 1,300 titles, making the widest range of the best books ever written available to millions – and constantly redefining the meaning of what makes a 'classic'.

The Odyssey continues ...

The best books ever written

PENGUIN (A) CLASSICS

SINCE 1946